Mastering Python Serverless Framework

Build and Deploy Scalable Applications with Ease. A Python Developer's Guide!

Katie Millie

Mastering Python Serverless Framework

Build and Deploy Scalable Applications with Ease. A Python Developer's Guide!

By

Katie Millie

Copyright notice

Copyright © 2024 Katie Millie. All Rights Reserved.

Unauthorized use or reproduction of this material, in any form, without the explicit and written consent of the author or owner of this site, is strictly forbidden. However, excerpts and links to the material are allowed, provided that proper and clear attribution is given to Katie Millie, with accurate and specific references to the original content.

This work is safeguarded by international copyright laws. The author retains the right to take legal action against any unauthorized use. Redistribution or reproduction, whether in electronic or mechanical formats—including photocopying, recording, or any system used for information storage and retrieval—is prohibited without prior written consent from the author.

The purpose of this copyright notice is to protect the intellectual property rights of Katie Millie and to preserve the integrity of the creative works. By adhering to this notice, you support the ongoing creation and dissemination of high-quality content. Thank you for your understanding and cooperation.

Table of Contents

INTRODUCTION

Chapter 1

    The Rise of Serverless Computing: Why Python and Serverless Frameworks are a Perfect Match

        Unleashing Agility and Cost-efficiency: The Benefits of Using a Serverless Framework

            A Roadmap for Success: What You'll Learn in This Book

Chapter 2

    What are Serverless Frameworks? Key Features and Benefits

        Comparing Popular Serverless Frameworks: Serverless Framework vs. AWS SAM and Others

            Choosing the Right Serverless Framework for Your Python Project

Chapter 3

    Mastering Python Serverless Framework: Setting Up Your Development Environment

        Understanding the Serverless Framework Project Structure: Configuration Files and Code Organization

            Writing Your First Serverless Function with Python: A Hands-on Example

Chapter 4

Creating Powerful Serverless Functions: The Building Blocks of Your Applications

Handling Different Types of Events: HTTP Requests, Queues, and More

Advanced Function Design: Asynchronous Programming, Caching Strategies, and Error Handling

Chapter 5

Understanding Event Sources and Triggers for Your Functions: APIs, Queues, and More

Building Event-Driven Workflows: Chaining Functions, Handling Complex Logic, and Fan-Out Patterns

Implementing Message Queues with SQS for Asynchronous Processing and Decoupling Functions

Chapter 6

Leveraging the Power of AWS Services: S3, DynamoDB, Lambda Layers, and Beyond

Building Serverless APIs with API Gateway: Exposing Your Functions to the World

Stream Processing with AWS Kinesis: Real-Time Data Analysis with Python Lambdas and Serverless Framework

Chapter 7

Understanding Different Deployment Strategies: Local Testing, Staging Environments, and Production Deployments

Deploying Your Serverless Application to AWS

with Serverless Framework: Configuration and Best Practices

Managing Your Serverless Resources: Monitoring, Logging, Cost Optimization, and Version Control

Chapter 8

Unit Testing Your Python Functions: Ensuring Code Quality and Functionality

Debugging Serverless Applications: Techniques for Identifying and Fixing Issues

Advanced Debugging Strategies: Utilizing CloudWatch Logs, X-Ray Tracing, and Debugging Tools

Chapter 9

Securing Your Serverless Functions: Authentication, Authorization, and Encryption

Best Practices for Secure Development: Protecting Your Code, Data, and APIs

Compliance Considerations: Building Secure Serverless Applications in Regulated Industries

Chapter 10

Serverless on the Edge: Bringing Computing Closer to the Data with Lambda@Edge

Serverless Machine Learning: Using Serverless Frameworks for AI/ML Workloads

Continuous Integration and Delivery (CI/CD) for Serverless Applications

Serverless Microservices Architecture:

> > Building Scalable and Agile Systems

Chapter 11
> Implementing Best Practices for Code Reusability, Efficiency, Maintainability, and Observability
> > Common Serverless Design Patterns: Strategies for Building Scalable and Reliable Applications
> > > Advanced Error Handling and State Management Techniques in Serverless Functions

Chapter 12
> Building real-time applications with WebSockets and serverless.
> > Implementing GraphQL APIs in a serverless architecture.
> > > Using serverless for machine learning model deployment.
> > > > Handling multi-region deployments and global applications.

Chapter 13
> Case Studies and Real-World Examples
> > Practical examples of common serverless use cases, such as chatbots, image processing, and IoT.

Chapter 14
> Planning and strategizing your migration.
> > Incremental migration techniques and best practices.
> > > Common challenges and how to address

them.
- Tools and frameworks to facilitate migration.

Conclusion

Appendix
- A: Glossary of Serverless Terms
- B: Serverless Framework Configuration Options (YAML and Python)
- C: Troubleshooting Common Serverless Framework Issues
- D: Best Practices Checklist for Python Serverless Development

INTRODUCTION

Mastering Python Serverless Framework: Unleash the Power of Serverless with Pythonic Grace

Calling all Pythonistas! Are you tired of wrestling with complex server setups and endless infrastructure woes? Do you dream of a world where your Python code can soar through the cloud, scaling effortlessly and freeing you to focus on what you do best – crafting innovative applications? Welcome to the electrifying realm of serverless computing, and **Mastering Python Serverless Framework** is your key to unlocking its full potential.

Forget the days of battling server provisioning, grappling with complex configurations, and constantly worrying about scaling bottlenecks. Serverless computing is a revolutionary paradigm shift, and **Mastering Python Serverless Framework** puts you in the driver's seat. Here's the magic trick: with this powerful framework, your Python code transforms into serverless functions – lightweight, on-demand powerhouses that execute only when needed.

Imagine a battalion of highly skilled Python ninjas, ready to spring into action at a moment's notice, then vanishing without a trace once their mission is complete. That's the beauty of serverless – efficiency and agility at their finest! But serverless isn't just about convenience; it unlocks a treasure trove of benefits for Python developers:

- **Unmatched Scalability:** Serverless scales seamlessly, automatically adjusting resources based on demand. No more sleepless nights worrying about server capacity – your Python applications soar effortlessly, handling surges in traffic with grace.
- **Cost Efficiency Unleashed:** Serverless is a pay-per-use model, meaning you only pay for the resources your functions consume. No more wasting money on idle servers – Python Serverless Framework lets you focus on building value, not burning a hole in your wallet.
- **Agile Development on Steroids:** Say goodbye to lengthy server setup and management. Python Serverless Framework streamlines your development workflow, allowing you to deploy your code faster than ever before. Get your innovative ideas to market in record time!

Mastering Python Serverless Framework equips you with the tools and techniques to become a master serverless Python developer:

- **Craft Flawless Functions:** Learn the art of writing clean, concise, and highly efficient Python functions for serverless deployment.

Unleash the full potential of your Python code, optimized for the serverless landscape.

- **Event-Driven Architecture Demystified:** Master the language of serverless – event-driven communication. Design your applications to react to events in real-time, creating highly responsive and dynamic systems. Imagine your Python code elegantly responding to the flow of data, like a conductor directing an orchestra of events.
- **Integration Nirvana:** Learn how to seamlessly integrate your serverless functions with other AWS services like S3, DynamoDB, and API Gateway. Build powerful cloud applications with effortless communication between your Python code and the vast AWS ecosystem.
- **Effortless Deployment and Management:** Discover the secrets of deploying and managing your serverless Python applications with ease. Utilize the power of Python Serverless Framework to streamline your workflow and automate tedious tasks.
- **Testing and Debugging Made Easy:** Uncover powerful techniques for testing and debugging your serverless functions. Ensure your Python code runs flawlessly in the serverless environment, eliminating bugs and ensuring exceptional performance.

Mastering Python Serverless Framework isn't just about theory; it's a practical guide packed with real-world code examples,battle-tested strategies, and enough information to get your hands dirty and start building. Whether you're a seasoned Python developer or just starting your serverless journey, this book is your key to unlocking the full potential of Python in the serverless world.

Are you ready to break free from the shackles of traditional Python development and join the serverless revolution? Don't wait! Grab your copy of **Mastering Python Serverless Framework** today, and watch your Python code soar to new heights in the electrifying world of serverless computing!

Chapter 1

The Rise of Serverless Computing: Why Python and Serverless Frameworks are a Perfect Match

Serverless computing has revolutionized the way developers build and deploy applications. By abstracting away the complexities of server management, serverless architecture allows developers to focus purely on code and business logic. Among the various languages that have thrived in this new paradigm, Python stands out due to its simplicity, readability, and the rich ecosystem it offers. This essay explores the rise of serverless computing and delves into why Python, particularly when combined with serverless frameworks, is an ideal match for this computing model.

The Evolution of Serverless Computing

Serverless computing, despite its name, does not mean that servers are not involved. Instead, it implies that developers do not have to manage the underlying servers. This computing model gained prominence with the introduction of AWS Lambda in 2014, which allowed developers to run code without provisioning or managing servers. The serverless architecture operates on the principle of Function-as-a-Service (FaaS), where code is executed in response to events, and the cloud provider automatically handles the scaling and execution of these functions.

Advantages of Serverless Computing

The serverless model offers several advantages:

1. Scalability: Serverless applications automatically scale with the number of requests. This means developers don't need to worry about manually scaling their infrastructure to handle varying loads.

2. Cost Efficiency: In a serverless architecture, you only pay for the computer time you consume. This is in contrast to traditional models where servers must be kept running regardless of the demand.

3. Reduced Operational Overhead: Developers can focus on writing code without worrying about server maintenance, patching, or capacity planning.

4. Faster Time-to-Market: By eliminating the need to manage infrastructure, developers can rapidly prototype and deploy applications, leading to quicker iterations and innovations.

Python: A Language Tailored for Serverless

Python has become one of the most popular programming languages globally, and its characteristics make it exceptionally well-suited for serverless computing:

1. Simplicity and Readability: Python's syntax is clean and easy to understand, which speeds up the development process. This is particularly beneficial in serverless environments where quick deployments and iterations are common.

2. Rich Ecosystem: Python boasts a vast ecosystem of libraries and frameworks. For serverless computing, libraries such as Boto3 for AWS services, Flask for microservices, and Django for web applications can be seamlessly integrated.

3. Versatility: Python is versatile and can be used for various tasks, from web development to data analysis, machine learning, and automation. This versatility allows developers to use a single language across different parts of their serverless applications.

4. Community and Support: Python has a robust and active community. This means extensive documentation, numerous tutorials, and a wealth of third-party tools and libraries that can facilitate serverless development.

Serverless Frameworks and Python

Several frameworks have been developed to simplify the creation and management of serverless applications. One of the most prominent is the Serverless Framework, which is an open-source framework that allows developers to build and deploy serverless applications with ease.

The Serverless Framework

The Serverless Framework provides a powerful abstraction over cloud provider APIs. It supports multiple cloud providers, including AWS, Azure, and Google Cloud, allowing for a provider-agnostic development experience. Here's why the Serverless Framework is a perfect match for Python:

1. Ease of Use: The Serverless Framework abstracts much of the complexity involved in deploying serverless applications. With simple configuration files written in YAML, developers can define their functions, events, and resources without delving into intricate details of the cloud provider's API.

2. Integration with Python: The Serverless Framework seamlessly integrates with Python, enabling developers to write their functions in Python and deploy them effortlessly. It automatically handles the packaging of Python dependencies, which can often be a challenging aspect of deploying Python applications in a serverless environment.

3. Plugin Ecosystem: The Serverless Framework has a rich plugin ecosystem that extends its capabilities. For Python developers, plugins such as serverless-python-requirements can simplify dependency management by automatically packaging and deploying Python dependencies.

4. Local Development and Testing: The framework supports local development and testing, allowing developers to simulate the cloud environment on their local machines. This capability is crucial for Python developers who rely on a rapid development cycle.

Example Workflow with Python and the Serverless Framework

Here is a typical workflow for developing a serverless application using Python and the Serverless Framework:

1. Setup: Install the Serverless Framework and initialize a new project.

```sh
npm install -g serverless
serverless create --template aws-python3 --path my-service
cd my-service
```

2. Define Functions and Events: In the `serverless.yml` configuration file, define your functions and the events that trigger them.

```yaml
service: my-service
```

```
provider:
  name: aws
  runtime: python3.8

functions:
  hello:
    handler: handler.hello
    events:
      - http:
          path: hello
          method: get
```

3. Write Code: Implement your functions in Python.

```python
def hello(event, context):
    return {
        "statusCode": 200,
        "body": "Hello, world!"
    }
```

4. Deploy: Deploy the application to the cloud provider.

```sh
serverless deploy
```

5. Invoke and Test: Test your function either via the web interface or using the Serverless Framework CLI.

```sh
serverless invoke -f hello
```

Use Cases for Python in Serverless

Python's versatility makes it suitable for a wide range of serverless applications:

1. Web Applications and APIs: Using frameworks like Flask or Django, Python developers can build robust web applications and APIs that scale automatically in a serverless environment.

2. Data Processing and ETL: Python is a preferred language for data processing tasks. Serverless architectures allow for efficient and scalable ETL (Extract, Transform, Load) processes.

3. Machine Learning: Python's dominance in the machine learning space, thanks to libraries like TensorFlow and scikit-learn, makes it a natural fit for deploying machine learning models in a serverless fashion.

4. Automation and Scripting: Python's ease of use for scripting and automation can be leveraged in serverless functions to perform tasks like file processing, database management, and integration with third-party services.

Challenges and Considerations

While the combination of Python and serverless frameworks offers numerous benefits, there are also challenges and considerations:

1. Cold Starts: Serverless functions can experience latency during cold starts, which is the initial delay when a function is invoked after being idle. This can be mitigated with strategies like warming up functions or using provisioned concurrency.

2. State Management: Serverless functions are stateless by design. Managing state across function invocations requires careful consideration, often involving external storage solutions like databases or caches.

3. Monitoring and Debugging: Debugging serverless applications can be more complex compared to traditional applications. Effective logging, monitoring, and tracing are crucial for maintaining the health of serverless applications.

The rise of serverless computing marks a significant shift in how applications are developed and deployed. By abstracting the underlying infrastructure, serverless architectures empower developers to focus on code and innovation. Python's simplicity, versatility, and extensive ecosystem make it a perfect match for serverless computing. When combined with frameworks like the Serverless Framework, Python developers can rapidly build, deploy, and scale applications, unlocking new levels of productivity and efficiency. As serverless computing continues to evolve, the synergy between Python and serverless frameworks will undoubtedly play a pivotal role in shaping the future of cloud computing.

Unleashing Agility and Cost-efficiency: The Benefits of Using a Serverless Framework

The rise of cloud computing has brought about several paradigms that have revolutionized the way applications are developed and deployed. Among these, serverless computing stands out for its promise of agility and cost-efficiency. A serverless framework allows developers to focus on writing code while the cloud provider manages the infrastructure. Python, with its simplicity and robustness, has emerged as a preferred language for serverless applications. This essay explores the benefits of using a serverless framework, particularly in the context of Python, and how it unleashes agility and cost-efficiency in modern software development.

The Concept of Serverless Computing

Serverless computing, despite the misleading name, involves servers, but the key difference lies in how these servers are managed. In a traditional server-based model, developers need to provision, manage, and scale servers. In contrast, serverless computing abstracts these responsibilities to the cloud provider. Developers write functions that are triggered by events, and the cloud provider handles the execution, scaling, and infrastructure management.

Agility in Development

Rapid Development and Deployment

One of the primary advantages of using a serverless framework is the acceleration of the development and deployment cycle. With serverless, developers can quickly write and deploy functions without worrying about the underlying infrastructure. This rapid iteration capability is crucial in today's fast-paced development environments where time-to-market is a competitive advantage.

For example, using the Serverless Framework with Python, developers can set up a new project, define functions, and deploy them to the cloud within minutes. The Serverless Framework provides a high level of abstraction, allowing developers to focus on business logic rather than configuration and deployment details.

```sh
npm install -g serverless
serverless create --template aws-python3 --path my-service
cd my-service
serverless deploy
```

Flexibility and Scalability

Serverless computing offers unparalleled flexibility. Developers can create microservices architectures where each function performs a specific task, promoting modular and maintainable codebases. This approach aligns with modern software development practices such as Continuous Integration and Continuous Deployment (CI/CD), where small, incremental changes are tested and deployed frequently.

Scalability is another critical aspect of agility. Serverless functions automatically scale with the number of incoming requests. This means developers don't need to worry about provisioning additional servers or managing load balancers. The cloud provider dynamically allocates resources to handle the load, ensuring consistent performance.

Cost-efficiency

Pay-as-You-Go Pricing Model

Serverless computing introduces a pay-as-you-go pricing model, which significantly reduces costs. In traditional server-based models, organizations often have to over-provision resources to handle peak loads, leading to underutilized servers and wasted money. With serverless, you only pay for the actual compute time your functions use.

For instance, AWS Lambda charges are based on the number of requests and the execution duration. This model ensures that you are not paying for idle resources. Python's efficiency and performance, combined with the Serverless Framework's optimization features, can further minimize costs by reducing execution time.

Reduced Operational Costs

By offloading server management to the cloud provider, serverless computing reduces operational costs. There's no need for teams of system administrators to manage servers, apply patches, or handle capacity planning. This reduction in operational overhead allows organizations to allocate resources to other critical areas, such as development and innovation.

The Serverless Framework enhances this cost-efficiency by simplifying the deployment process and providing built-in tools for monitoring and managing serverless applications. Plugins like `serverless-plugin-cost-savings` help developers optimize their functions to reduce costs further.

Enhancing Developer Productivity

Simplified Management and Configuration

The Serverless Framework simplifies the management and configuration of serverless applications. Using declarative configuration files written in YAML, developers can define their functions, events, and resources in a straightforward manner. This approach reduces the cognitive load on developers, allowing them to focus on coding rather than infrastructure management.

```yaml
service: my-service

provider:
  name: aws
  runtime: python3.8

functions:
  hello:
    handler: handler.hello
    events:
      - http:
```

         path: hello
         method: get

Extensive Plugin Ecosystem

The Serverless Framework has a rich plugin ecosystem that extends its capabilities. Plugins can automate various tasks, such as packaging dependencies, optimizing functions, and integrating with other services. For Python developers, plugins like `serverless-python-requirements` make it easy to package and deploy dependencies, ensuring that functions run smoothly in the cloud environment.

Local Development and Testing

Developers often face challenges when developing and testing serverless functions locally. The Serverless Framework addresses this issue by providing tools for local development and testing. For example, the `serverless-offline` plugin allows developers to simulate AWS Lambda and API Gateway locally, enabling them to test their functions without deploying to the cloud.

```sh
sls offline
```

This capability speeds up the development process, as developers can quickly iterate on their code and identify issues before deploying to production.

Real-world Use Cases

Web Applications and APIs

Serverless computing is ideal for building scalable web applications and APIs. Using frameworks like Flask or Django, Python developers can create robust web services that automatically scale based on demand. The Serverless Framework simplifies the deployment and management of these applications, ensuring high availability and performance.

For example, a Flask-based API can be deployed using the Serverless Framework with minimal configuration. The framework handles the setup of API Gateway, Lambda functions, and other necessary resources, allowing developers to focus on their application logic.

Data Processing and ETL

Python's strength in data processing makes it a natural fit for serverless architectures. Serverless functions can be used for Extract, Transform, Load (ETL) processes, where data is ingested, transformed, and stored in a scalable and cost-efficient manner. The Serverless Framework can orchestrate these tasks, ensuring that data pipelines run smoothly and efficiently.

Machine Learning and AI

Python is the language of choice for machine learning and AI, thanks to libraries like TensorFlow, PyTorch, and scikit-learn. Serverless computing allows developers to deploy machine learning models as serverless functions, making it easy to scale predictions and inference tasks. The Serverless Framework simplifies the deployment and management of these models, enabling rapid experimentation and iteration.

For instance, a machine learning model can be packaged as a serverless function that processes input data and returns predictions. This function can be triggered by events such as HTTP requests, data uploads, or scheduled jobs, ensuring flexibility and scalability.

Challenges and Best Practices

While serverless computing offers numerous benefits, it also presents certain challenges. Cold starts, state management, and debugging can be more complex compared to traditional architectures. However, these challenges can be mitigated with best practices and tools provided by the Serverless Framework.

Cold Starts

Cold starts occur when a serverless function is invoked after being idle, leading to increased latency. Strategies to mitigate cold starts include provisioning concurrency, warming up functions, and optimizing function performance.

State Management

Serverless functions are stateless by design, which can complicate state management across function invocations. Solutions include using external storage services like Amazon S3, DynamoDB, or Redis to maintain state.

Monitoring and Debugging

Effective monitoring and debugging are crucial for maintaining the health of serverless applications. The Serverless Framework integrates with monitoring tools like AWS CloudWatch and provides plugins for enhanced logging and tracing.

The adoption of serverless computing is transforming the landscape of software development. By abstracting away the complexities of infrastructure management, serverless frameworks like the Serverless Framework unleash agility and cost-efficiency, enabling developers to focus on delivering value through their applications. Python's simplicity, versatility, and robust ecosystem make it an ideal language for serverless development. The combination of Python and the Serverless Framework empowers developers to build scalable, cost-effective, and high-performance applications, driving innovation and accelerating time-to-market in the competitive world of technology.

A Roadmap for Success: What You'll Learn in This Book

Welcome to "Mastering Python Serverless Frameworks"! This book is your comprehensive guide to understanding and harnessing the power of serverless computing using Python and the Serverless Framework. Whether you're a seasoned developer looking to expand your skill set or a beginner eager to dive into the world of serverless, this book will equip you with the knowledge and tools you need to succeed. Here's what you can expect to learn as you journey through the chapters.

Chapter 1: Introduction to Serverless Computing

We begin with the fundamentals, explaining what serverless computing is and how it differs from traditional and other cloud-based models. You'll learn about:

- The evolution of serverless computing.

- Key concepts such as Function-as-a-Service (FaaS) and Backend-as-a-Service (BaaS).

- The benefits and challenges of adopting a serverless architecture.

- An overview of leading serverless providers like AWS Lambda, Azure Functions, and Google Cloud Functions.

Chapter 2: Setting Up Your Development Environment

Before diving into code, it's essential to set up your environment. This chapter will guide you through:

- Installing Python and the necessary development tools.

- Setting up a virtual environment to manage dependencies.

- Installing the Serverless Framework and configuring it for your chosen cloud provider.

- Basic command-line operations in the Serverless Framework.

Chapter 3: Your First Serverless Function

Here, you'll get hands-on experience by creating, deploying, and testing your first serverless function. You'll learn:

- How to create a new Serverless Framework project.

- Writing a simple "Hello, World!" function in Python.

- Defining events that trigger your function (HTTP requests, scheduled tasks, etc.).

- Deploying your function to the cloud and invoking it.

Chapter 4: Deep Dive into the Serverless Framework

Understanding the full capabilities of the Serverless Framework is crucial for building robust applications. This chapter covers:

- Detailed configuration of `serverless.yml`.

- Managing environments and stages (development, production, etc.).

- Using variables and secrets securely.

- Customizing resource configurations for optimal performance.

Chapter 5: Building RESTful APIs with Flask and Serverless

Serverless is ideal for building scalable APIs. In this chapter, you'll learn:

- Setting up a Flask application within a serverless framework.

- Routing and handling HTTP requests in Flask.

- Deploying a Flask-based serverless API.

- Managing API Gateway and Lambda integration.

Chapter 6: Working with Databases in a Serverless Environment

Data persistence is a critical aspect of most applications. This chapter explores:

- Connecting serverless functions to databases (relational and NoSQL).

- Using AWS DynamoDB for a fully serverless database solution.

- Managing database connections and transactions in serverless functions.

- Strategies for efficient data access and storage.

Chapter 7: Asynchronous Processing and Event-Driven Architectures

Serverless excels in handling asynchronous and event-driven workflows. You'll discover:

- Setting up and handling event sources like S3, SNS, and SQS.

- Writing functions that respond to events and process data asynchronously.

- Chaining functions together to create workflows using Step Functions.

- Designing for idempotency and error handling in event-driven systems.

Chapter 8: Security and Best Practices

Security is paramount in any application. This chapter focuses on:

- Implementing authentication and authorization in serverless applications.

- Using AWS IAM roles and policies for fine-grained access control.

- Securing sensitive data and managing environment variables.

- Best practices for coding, deploying, and maintaining secure serverless applications.

Chapter 9: Monitoring and Debugging

Monitoring and debugging serverless applications can be challenging. This chapter provides tools and techniques for:

- Setting up logging and monitoring with AWS CloudWatch.

- Using third-party monitoring solutions like Datadog and New Relic.

- Debugging serverless functions locally and in the cloud.

- Handling and analyzing errors and performance bottlenecks.

Chapter 10: Testing Serverless Applications

Ensuring the reliability of your serverless applications requires robust testing strategies. You'll learn about:

- Unit testing and integration testing for serverless functions.

- Mocking and simulating cloud services in tests.

- Automated testing with CI/CD pipelines.

- Using frameworks and tools like pytest and Serverless Offline for testing.

Chapter 11: Advanced Topics in Serverless

To push your serverless skills further, this chapter covers advanced topics such as:

- Building real-time applications with WebSockets and serverless.

- Implementing GraphQL APIs in a serverless architecture.

- Using serverless for machine learning model deployment.

- Handling multi-region deployments and global applications.

Chapter 12: Case Studies and Real-World Examples

Learning from real-world applications can provide valuable insights. This chapter presents:

- Detailed case studies of successful serverless implementations.

- Lessons learned from real-world projects.

- Practical examples of common serverless use cases, such as chatbots, image processing, and IoT.

Chapter 13: Optimizing and Scaling Serverless Applications

Optimizing performance and cost efficiency is critical in serverless applications. You'll explore:

- Techniques for reducing cold start latency.
- Efficient resource and dependency management.
- Cost optimization strategies and monitoring.
- Scaling strategies for high-throughput applications.

Chapter 14: Migration to Serverless

If you're transitioning from a traditional or other cloud-based architecture to serverless, this chapter will guide you through:

- Planning and strategizing your migration.

- Incremental migration techniques and best practices.

- Common challenges and how to address them.

- Tools and frameworks to facilitate migration.

Chapter 15: Future Trends in Serverless Computing

The serverless landscape is continually evolving. In the final chapter, you'll look at:

- Emerging trends and technologies in serverless computing.

- The future of serverless and its impact on software development.

- How to stay updated and continue learning in the fast-paced world of serverless.

"Mastering Python Serverless Frameworks" is designed to be your comprehensive resource for mastering serverless computing with Python. By the end of this book, you will have a thorough understanding of how to build, deploy, and manage serverless applications. You will be equipped with the skills to leverage the full power of serverless architecture, ensuring agility, scalability, and cost-efficiency in your software projects. Whether you're building simple functions or complex, event-driven systems, this book will guide you every step of the way, providing practical insights and real-world examples to help you succeed.

Chapter 2

What are Serverless Frameworks? Key Features and Benefits

Serverless computing has revolutionized the way developers build and deploy applications, allowing them to focus on writing code without worrying about the underlying infrastructure. The serverless model abstracts server management, scaling, and maintenance, enabling developers to deploy functions directly in the cloud. This paradigm shift has given rise to several serverless frameworks, each designed to simplify the development and deployment of serverless applications. One of the most prominent frameworks in this domain is the Serverless Framework, especially popular in the context of AWS Lambda.

What are Serverless Frameworks?

Serverless frameworks are tools and libraries that assist developers in building, deploying, and managing serverless applications. These frameworks provide a structured approach to creating serverless functions, managing resources, and automating deployment processes. By using a serverless framework, developers can define their functions, configure the required cloud services, and deploy their applications with minimal effort.

The Serverless Framework, often referred to simply as "Serverless," is one of the most widely used serverless frameworks. It supports multiple cloud providers, including AWS, Azure, Google Cloud, and more, making it versatile and powerful.

Key Features of the Serverless Framework

1. Multi-Provider Support: Serverless Framework supports various cloud providers, allowing developers to write provider-agnostic code. This feature is beneficial for organizations that use multiple cloud services or plan to switch providers.

2. Infrastructure as Code (IaC): With Serverless, developers define the infrastructure required for their application in configuration files (YAML or JSON). This approach ensures that infrastructure changes are version-controlled and reproducible.

3. Simplified Deployment: The framework abstracts the complexities of deployment, allowing developers to deploy their functions and associated resources with a single command. It handles resource provisioning, function packaging, and deployment.

4. Extensibility through Plugins: Serverless Framework has a rich ecosystem of plugins that extend its functionality. Developers can use existing plugins or create custom ones to tailor the deployment process to their needs.

5. Event-Driven Architecture: Serverless applications are often event-driven, and the Serverless Framework makes it easy to define triggers and events that invoke functions. These can include HTTP requests, scheduled events, or cloud service events.

6. Local Development and Testing: The framework provides tools for local development and testing, enabling developers to simulate the cloud environment on their local machines.

7. Monitoring and Debugging: Integrated tools and plugins provide monitoring and debugging capabilities, helping developers track the performance and health of their serverless applications.

Benefits of Using the Serverless Framework

1. Reduced Operational Complexity: By abstracting server management, the Serverless Framework allows developers to focus on writing code rather than managing infrastructure. This reduces operational overhead and simplifies the development process.

2. Cost Efficiency: Serverless computing follows a pay-as-you-go model, where you only pay for the compute time your functions consume. This can lead to significant cost savings, especially for applications with variable or unpredictable workloads.

3. Scalability: Serverless functions automatically scale with demand, ensuring that applications can handle varying levels of traffic without manual intervention. This feature is particularly useful for applications with spiky traffic patterns.

4. Rapid Development and Deployment: The framework's abstraction and automation features enable rapid development and deployment cycles. Developers can quickly iterate on their functions and deploy updates with minimal downtime.

5. Enhanced Productivity: With the serverless model and tools like the Serverless Framework, developers can build and deploy applications faster, improving overall productivity and reducing time-to-market.

Getting Started with the Serverless Framework and Python

To illustrate how to use the Serverless Framework, let's walk through a simple example of creating, deploying, and testing a serverless application using Python.

Prerequisites

- Node.js and npm installed

- Serverless Framework installed (`npm install -g serverless`)

- AWS CLI configured with appropriate permissions

- Python installed

Step-by-Step Guide

1. Create a New Serverless Project

```bash
serverless create --template aws-python3 --path my-serverless-app
cd my-serverless-app
```

This command creates a new Serverless project using the `aws-python3` template, setting up the basic structure for a Python-based serverless application.

2. Define the Serverless Configuration

Open the `serverless.yml` file and define your service, provider, and functions. Here's a simple example:

```yaml
service: my-serverless-app

provider:
  name: aws
  runtime: python3.8
  region: us-east-1

functions:
```

```
hello:
  handler: handler.hello
  events:
    - http:
        path: hello
        method: get
```

This configuration defines a single function named `hello` that will be triggered by an HTTP GET request to the `/hello` path.

3. Implement the Function

Open the `handler.py` file and implement the `hello` function:

```python
def hello(event, context):
    body = {
        "message": "Hello, World!",
        "input": event
    }
    response = {
        "statusCode": 200,
        "body": json.dumps(body)
    }
```

        return response
```

This simple function returns a JSON response with a greeting message.

**4. Deploy the Application**

Deploy your serverless application to AWS:

```bash
serverless deploy
```

The Serverless Framework will package your code, create the necessary AWS resources, and deploy the function. After deployment, you'll receive a URL for the HTTP endpoint.

5. Invoke the Function

You can test the deployed function by making an HTTP GET request to the provided endpoint or using the Serverless Framework CLI:

```bash

```
serverless invoke -f hello -l
```

This command invokes the `hello` function and outputs the logs.

6. Monitoring and Debugging

After deployment, you can monitor your function using AWS CloudWatch. The Serverless Framework also supports additional monitoring tools through plugins.

Advanced Features

For more advanced use cases, the Serverless Framework supports:

- **Environment Variables:** Securely pass environment variables to your functions.

```yaml
provider:
  ...
  environment:
    MY_VAR: "my-value"
```

- **Resource Management:** Define custom AWS resources in the `serverless.yml` file.

```yaml
resources:
  Resources:
    MyTable:
      Type: AWS::DynamoDB::Table
      Properties:
        TableName: MyTable
        AttributeDefinitions:
          - AttributeName: id
            AttributeType: S
        KeySchema:
          - AttributeName: id
            KeyType: HASH
        ProvisionedThroughput:
          ReadCapacityUnits: 1
          WriteCapacityUnits: 1
```

- **Custom Plugins:** Extend the framework's functionality by writing custom plugins.

```javascript
class MyPlugin {
```

```
  constructor(serverless, options) {
    this.serverless = serverless;
    this.options = options;

    this.hooks = {
      'before:deploy:deploy':
this.beforeDeploy.bind(this),
    };

    beforeDeploy() {
      this.serverless.cli.log('Hello from my plugin!');
    }
  module.exports = MyPlugin;
```

The Serverless Framework simplifies the development, deployment, and management of serverless applications. Its key features, such as multi-provider support, infrastructure as code, and extensibility through plugins, make it a powerful tool for developers. By reducing operational complexity, improving cost efficiency, and enabling rapid development, the Serverless Framework empowers developers to build scalable and reliable serverless applications with ease.

For those looking to master the Serverless Framework, a deep dive into its configuration options, plugin system, and integration with other cloud services is essential. With the right knowledge and tools, developers can leverage serverless computing to deliver innovative and efficient solutions.

Comparing Popular Serverless Frameworks: Serverless Framework vs. AWS SAM and Others

Serverless computing has rapidly gained popularity, enabling developers to focus on writing code without managing the underlying infrastructure. Various frameworks have emerged to facilitate the development and deployment of serverless applications. Among them, the Serverless Framework and AWS Serverless Application Model (SAM) are two of the most prominent. This article compares these frameworks and others, such as Google Cloud Functions Framework and Azure Functions, focusing on their features, benefits, and use cases, with a particular emphasis on using Python.

Serverless Framework

Overview

The Serverless Framework is an open-source framework that simplifies the deployment of serverless applications. It supports multiple cloud providers, including AWS, Azure, Google Cloud, and more. The framework abstracts infrastructure management, allowing developers to define their serverless applications in a configuration file and deploy them with a single command.

Key Features

1. Multi-Provider Support: The Serverless Framework supports various cloud providers, making it highly versatile.

2. Infrastructure as Code (IaC): Define infrastructure in YAML or JSON configuration files, ensuring version control and reproducibility.

3. Extensibility through Plugins: A rich ecosystem of plugins extends functionality, and custom plugins can be created as needed.

4. Event-Driven Architecture: Easily define triggers and events to invoke functions.

5. Local Development and Testing: Tools for local development and testing simulate the cloud environment.

Here is a simple example using the Serverless Framework with AWS Lambda and Python:

```bash
# Install Serverless Framework
npm install -g serverless

# Create a new Serverless service
serverless create --template aws-python3 --path my-serverless-app
cd my-serverless-app
```

Define the service in `serverless.yml`:

```yaml
service: my-serverless-app

provider:
  name: aws
  runtime: python3.8
  region: us-east-1
```

```yaml
functions:
  hello:
    handler: handler.hello
    events:
      - http:
          path: hello
          method: get
```

Implement the function in `handler.py`:

```python
import json

def hello(event, context):
    body = {
        "message": "Hello, World!",
        "input": event
    }
    response = {
        "statusCode": 200,
        "body": json.dumps(body)
    }
    return response
```

Deploy the application:

```bash
serverless deploy
```

AWS Serverless Application Model (SAM)

Overview

AWS SAM is an open-source framework designed specifically for building serverless applications on AWS. It extends AWS CloudFormation to provide a simplified way of defining AWS Lambda functions, API Gateway endpoints, DynamoDB tables, and other resources.

Key Features

1. Tight Integration with AWS Services: SAM is tailored for AWS, providing seamless integration with AWS services.

2. Simplified Syntax: SAM templates use a simplified syntax to define serverless resources, reducing boilerplate code.

3. Local Development and Testing: SAM CLI supports local invocation, debugging, and testing of Lambda functions.

4. Policy Templates: Built-in policy templates simplify the creation of IAM roles and policies.

Example

Here's an example using AWS SAM with Python:

```bash
# Install AWS SAM CLI
brew tap aws/tap
brew install aws-sam-cli

# Initialize a new SAM project
sam init --runtime python3.8 --name my-sam-app
cd my-sam-app
```

Define the function in `template.yaml`:

```yaml
AWSTemplateFormatVersion: '2010-09-09'
Transform: 'AWS::Serverless-2016-10-31'
```

```
Resources:
  HelloWorldFunction:
    Type: 'AWS::Serverless::Function'
    Properties:
      Handler: app.lambda_handler
      Runtime: python3.8
      Events:
        HelloWorld:
          Type: Api
          Properties:
            Path: /hello
            Method: get
```

Implement the function in `app.py`:

```python
import json

def lambda_handler(event, context):
    return {
        "statusCode": 200,
        "body": json.dumps({
            "message": "Hello, World!",
        }),
    }
```

Deploy the application:

```bash
sam build
sam deploy --guided
```

Google Cloud Functions Framework

Overview

Google Cloud Functions Framework allows developers to write and deploy serverless functions that run on Google Cloud. It supports various programming languages, including Python.

Key Features

1. Event-Driven Functions: Functions can be triggered by events from Google Cloud services, HTTP requests, and more.

2. Integrated Monitoring and Logging: Google Cloud provides integrated tools for monitoring and logging.

3. Local Development and Testing: Tools for local development and testing of functions before deployment.

Example

Here's an example using Google Cloud Functions with Python:

```bash
# Install Google Cloud SDK
curl https://sdk.cloud.google.com | bash

# Initialize a new project
gcloud init

# Create a new function
mkdir my-gcf-app
cd my-gcf-app
```

Define the function in `main.py`:

```python
def hello_world(request):
    return "Hello, World!"
```

Deploy the function:

```bash
gcloud functions deploy hello_world --runtime python39 --trigger-http --allow-unauthenticated
```

Azure Functions

Overview

Azure Functions is a serverless compute service that enables developers to run code on-demand without managing infrastructure. It supports a variety of programming languages, including Python.

Key Features

1. Event-Driven Execution: Functions can be triggered by events from Azure services, HTTP requests, and more.

2. Integrated Development Tools: Visual Studio and Visual Studio Code integration for developing, testing, and deploying functions.

3. Scalability: Automatic scaling based on demand.

Example

Here's an example using Azure Functions with Python:

```bash
# Install Azure Functions Core Tools
npm install -g azure-functions-core-tools@3

# Create a new function app
func init my-azure-app --python
cd my-azure-app

# Create a new function
func new --name HttpTrigger --template "HTTP trigger" --authlevel "anonymous"
```

Define the function in `HttpTrigger/__init__.py`:

```python
import logging
import azure.functions as func

def main(req: func.HttpRequest) -> func.HttpResponse:
    return func.HttpResponse("Hello, World!")
```

```

**Deploy the function:**

```bash
func azure functionapp publish <FunctionAppName>
```

Comparison and Use Cases

Multi-Provider Support

- **Serverless Framework:** Supports multiple providers (AWS, Azure, Google Cloud, etc.), making it ideal for multi-cloud strategies.

- **AWS SAM:** Exclusively designed for AWS, offering deep integration and simplified AWS resource management.

- **Google Cloud Functions Framework:** Best suited for applications that leverage Google Cloud services.

- **Azure Functions:** Ideal for applications within the Azure ecosystem.
```

Ease of Use

- **Serverless Framework:** Provides a user-friendly abstraction over multiple providers with extensive community support and plugins.

- **AWS SAM:** Simplifies AWS serverless development with a focus on reducing boilerplate and providing a native AWS experience.

- **Google Cloud Functions Framework:** Straightforward for developers familiar with Google Cloud.

- **Azure Functions:** Integrated with Azure tools and services, providing a seamless experience for Azure-centric development.

Local Development and Testing

- **Serverless Framework:** Strong support for local development and testing across multiple providers.

- **AWS SAM:** Excellent local development capabilities with SAM CLI.

- **Google Cloud Functions Framework:** Supports local testing with the Functions Framework.

- **Azure Functions:** Integrated tools for local development with Azure Functions Core Tools.

Choosing the right serverless framework depends on your specific needs, cloud provider preferences, and development workflow. The Serverless Framework offers versatility and multi-cloud support, making it a great choice for diverse environments. AWS SAM excels in AWS-centric projects with its deep integration and simplified syntax. Google Cloud Functions Framework and Azure Functions are tailored for their respective cloud ecosystems, providing seamless integration and robust support.

Mastering these frameworks involves understanding their unique features and use cases. By leveraging the strengths of each framework, developers can build efficient, scalable, and cost-effective serverless applications.

Choosing the Right Serverless Framework for Your Python Project

Serverless computing has significantly transformed the way developers build and deploy applications. By abstracting the server management, serverless frameworks allow developers to focus solely on writing code, which the cloud provider runs and scales automatically. However, choosing the right serverless framework for your Python project can be challenging due to the variety of options available, each with its strengths and unique features.

In this article, we'll explore several popular serverless frameworks, including the Serverless Framework, AWS Serverless Application Model (SAM), Google Cloud Functions Framework, and Azure Functions. We'll compare their features, use cases, and provide examples to help you make an informed decision for your Python project.

Serverless Framework

Overview

The Serverless Framework is an open-source framework that simplifies building and deploying serverless applications across various cloud providers such as AWS, Azure, Google Cloud, and more. It's highly extensible and supports a wide range of plugins, making it a versatile choice for multi-cloud environments.

Key Features

1. Multi-Provider Support: Supports AWS, Azure, Google Cloud, and others.

2. Infrastructure as Code (IaC): Use YAML or JSON to define your serverless application's infrastructure.

3. Extensibility through Plugins: A rich ecosystem of plugins to extend functionality.

4. Event-Driven Architecture: Easily define triggers and events to invoke functions.

5. Local Development and Testing: Tools to simulate the cloud environment locally.

Example

Here's how you can create and deploy a simple AWS Lambda function using the Serverless Framework and Python.

Step 1: Install the Serverless Framework

```bash
npm install -g serverless
```

Step 2: Create a New Serverless Service

```bash
serverless create --template aws-python3 --path my-serverless-app
cd my-serverless-app
```

Step 3: Define the Service in `serverless.yml`*

```yaml
service: my-serverless-app

provider:
  name: aws
  runtime: python3.8
```

```
  region: us-east-1

functions:
  hello:
    handler: handler.hello
    events:
      - http:
          path: hello
          method: get
```

Step 4: Implement the Function in `handler.py`

```python
import json

def hello(event, context):
    body = {
        "message": "Hello, World!",
        "input": event
    }
    response = {
        "statusCode": 200,
        "body": json.dumps(body)
    }

    return response
```

```

### Step 5: Deploy the Application

```bash
serverless deploy
```

AWS Serverless Application Model (SAM)

Overview

AWS SAM is an open-source framework specifically designed for building serverless applications on AWS. It extends AWS CloudFormation to provide a simplified way of defining AWS Lambda functions, API Gateway endpoints, DynamoDB tables, and more.

Key Features

1. Tight Integration with AWS Services: Seamless integration with AWS services.

2. Simplified Syntax: SAM templates use a simplified syntax to define serverless resources, reducing boilerplate code.
```

3. Local Development and Testing: SAM CLI supports local invocation, debugging, and testing of Lambda functions.

4. Policy Templates: Built-in policy templates simplify the creation of IAM roles and policies.

Example

Here's an example using AWS SAM with Python.

Step 1: Install AWS SAM CLI

```bash
brew tap aws/tap
brew install aws-sam-cli
```

Step 2: Initialize a New SAM Project

```bash
sam init --runtime python3.8 --name my-sam-app
cd my-sam-app
```

Step 3: Define the Function in `template.yaml`

```yaml
AWSTemplateFormatVersion: '2010-09-09'
Transform: 'AWS::Serverless-2016-10-31'
Resources:
  HelloWorldFunction:
    Type: 'AWS::Serverless::Function'
    Properties:
      Handler: app.lambda_handler
      Runtime: python3.8
      Events:
        HelloWorld:
          Type: Api
          Properties:
            Path: /hello
            Method: get
```

Step 4: Implement the Function in `app.py`

```python
import json

def lambda_handler(event, context):
    return {
        "statusCode": 200,
```

```
        "body": json.dumps({
          "message": "Hello, World!",
        }),
```

Step 5: Deploy the Application

```bash
sam build
sam deploy --guided
```

Google Cloud Functions Framework

Overview

Google Cloud Functions Framework is designed to build and deploy serverless functions on Google Cloud. It supports multiple programming languages, including Python, and integrates well with Google Cloud services.

Key Features

1. Event-Driven Functions: Functions can be triggered by various events from Google Cloud services.

2. Integrated Monitoring and Logging: Google Cloud provides robust tools for monitoring and logging.

3. Local Development and Testing: Supports local testing before deployment.

Example

Here's an example using Google Cloud Functions with Python.

Step 1: Install Google Cloud SDK

```bash
curl https://sdk.cloud.google.com | bash
exec -l $SHELL
gcloud init
```

Step 2: Create a New Function

```bash
mkdir my-gcf-app
cd my-gcf-app
```

Step 3: Define the Function in `main.py`

```python
def hello_world(request):
    return "Hello, World!"
```

Step 4: Deploy the Function'

```bash
gcloud functions deploy hello_world --runtime python39 --trigger-http --allow-unauthenticated
```

Azure Functions

Overview

Azure Functions is a serverless compute service that enables you to run event-driven code without managing infrastructure. It integrates seamlessly with Azure services and supports a variety of programming languages, including Python.

Key Features

1. Event-Driven Execution: Functions can be triggered by events from Azure services, HTTP requests, and more.

2. Integrated Development Tools: Visual Studio and Visual Studio Code integration for developing, testing, and deploying functions.

3. Scalability: Automatically scales based on demand.

Example

Here's an example using Azure Functions with Python.

Step 1: Install Azure Functions Core Tools

```bash
npm install -g azure-functions-core-tools@3
```

Step 2: Create a New Function App

```bash
func init my-azure-app --python
cd my-azure-app
```

Step 3: Create a New Function

```bash
func new --name HttpTrigger --template "HTTP trigger" --authlevel "anonymous"
```

Step 4: Implement the Function in `HttpTrigger/__init__.py`

```python
import logging
import azure.functions as func

def main(req: func.HttpRequest) -> func.HttpResponse:
    return func.HttpResponse("Hello, World!")
```

Step 5: Deploy the Function

```bash
func azure functionapp publish <FunctionAppName>
```

Comparison and Choosing the Right Framework

Multi-Provider Support

- **Serverless Framework:** Best for multi-cloud strategies due to its broad support for various cloud providers.

- **AWS SAM:** Ideal for AWS-centric projects, offering deep integration with AWS services.

- **Google Cloud Functions Framework:** Suitable for projects leveraging Google Cloud services.

- **Azure Functions:** Best for applications within the Azure ecosystem.

Ease of Use

- **Serverless Framework:** User-friendly with extensive community support and plugins.

- **AWS SAM:** Simplifies AWS serverless development with a native AWS experience.

- **Google Cloud Functions Framework:** Straightforward for developers familiar with Google Cloud.

- **Azure Functions:** Integrated with Azure tools, providing a seamless development experience.

Local Development and Testing

- **Serverless Framework:** Strong support for local development and testing across multiple providers.

- **AWS SAM:** Excellent local development capabilities with SAM CLI.

- **Google Cloud Functions Framework:** Supports local testing with the Functions Framework.

- **Azure Functions:** Integrated tools for local development with Azure Functions Core Tools.

Deployment and Management

- **Serverless Framework:** Automates deployment and management across multiple providers.

- **AWS SAM:** Simplifies deployment with AWS CloudFormation templates.

- **Google Cloud Functions Framework:** Easy deployment with gcloud CLI.

- **Azure Functions:** Seamless deployment with Azure CLI and integrated development tools.

Choosing the right serverless framework for your Python project depends on your specific needs, cloud provider preferences, and development workflow. The Serverless Framework offers versatility and multi-cloud support, making it a great choice for diverse environments. AWS SAM excels in AWS-centric projects with its deep integration and simplified syntax. Google Cloud Functions Framework and Azure Functions are tailored for their respective cloud ecosystems, providing seamless integration and robust support.

By understanding the unique features and capabilities of each framework, you can make an informed decision that aligns with your project requirements and development goals. Whether you're looking for multi-provider support, ease of use, strong local development tools, or seamless deployment, there's a serverless framework that fits your needs.

Chapter 3

Mastering Python Serverless Framework: Setting Up Your Development Environment

Installing the Serverless Framework and Configuring Your Local Development Environment

Serverless computing allows developers to focus on writing code without worrying about the underlying infrastructure. The Serverless Framework simplifies this process by providing an easy-to-use toolkit for building and deploying serverless applications across multiple cloud providers. This guide will walk you through the steps to install the Serverless Framework and configure your local development environment, specifically for Python projects.

Prerequisites

Before installing the Serverless Framework, ensure that you have the following prerequisites:

1. Node.js and npm: The Serverless Framework is a Node.js application. You need to have Node.js and npm installed. You can download them from nodejs.org.

2. Python: Ensure you have Python installed. The Serverless Framework supports Python versions 3.6 and above. You can download Python from [python.org](https://www.python.org/downloads/).

3. AWS CLI: For deploying to AWS, you'll need the AWS CLI installed and configured. You can install it from the [AWS CLI User Guide](https://docs.aws.amazon.com/cli/latest/userguide/install-cliv2.html).

Step 1: Install Node.js and npm

If you don't already have Node.js and npm installed, download and install the latest LTS version from nodejs.org. Verify the installation by running the following commands:

```bash
node -v
npm -v
```

Step 2: Install the Serverless Framework

Once Node.js and npm are installed, you can install the Serverless Framework globally using npm:

```bash
npm install -g serverless
```

Verify the installation by running:

```bash
serverless --version
```

Step 3: Set Up Your AWS Credentials

To deploy serverless applications to AWS, you need to configure the AWS CLI with your credentials. If you haven't done so, follow these steps:

1. Install the AWS CLI from the [AWS CLI User Guide](https://docs.aws.amazon.com/cli/latest/userguide/install-cliv2.html).

2. Configure the AWS CLI with your credentials:

```bash
aws configure
```

You will be prompted to enter your AWS Access Key ID, Secret Access Key, region, and output format. You can find these details in the AWS Management Console under your account's security credentials.

Step 4: Create a New Serverless Project

With the Serverless Framework installed and your AWS credentials configured, you can create a new serverless project. Use the `serverless create` command to generate a new project structure:

```bash
serverless create --template aws-python3 --path my-serverless-app
cd my-serverless-app
```

This command creates a new directory called `my-serverless-app` with the following structure:

```
my-serverless-app/
├── handler.py
├── serverless.yml
└── .gitignore
```

Step 5: Define Your Serverless Service

The `serverless.yml` file is where you define your serverless service. This file contains the configuration for your functions, events, and resources. Here's an example `serverless.yml` file for a simple Hello World function:

```yaml
service: my-serverless-app

provider:
  name: aws
  runtime: python3.8
  region: us-east-1

functions:
  hello:
    handler: handler.hello
```

```
events:
  - http:
      path: hello
      method: get
```

Step 6: Implement Your Function

In the `handler.py` file, you can define the function logic. Here's a simple example of a Python function that returns a Hello World response:

```python
import json

def hello(event, context):
    body = {
        "message": "Hello, World!",
        "input": event
    }

    response = {
        "statusCode": 200,
        "body": json.dumps(body)
    }
```

    return response
```

**Step 7: Deploy Your Serverless Application**

With your function and configuration in place, you can deploy your serverless application to AWS using the following command:

```bash
serverless deploy
```

The deployment process will package your code, create the necessary AWS resources, and deploy your function. After the deployment is complete, you will see the endpoint URL for your function.

Step 8: Test Your Deployed Function

After deployment, you can test your function by sending a request to the endpoint URL provided in the deployment output. You can use `curl` or any API testing tool to send a request:

```bash

```
curl https://<your-api-id>.execute-api.us-east-1.amazonaws.com/dev/hello
```

You should receive a response similar to:

```json
{
  "message": "Hello, World!",
  "input": {
    // request details
  }
}
```

Step 9: Set Up Local Development and Testing

To improve your development workflow, the Serverless Framework provides tools for local development and testing. You can use the `serverless invoke local` command to invoke your function locally:

```bash
serverless invoke local --function hello
```

This command runs your function locally and prints the output, which helps in quick testing and debugging.

Step 10: Use Serverless Offline for Local API Development

For more extensive local development, you can use the `serverless-offline` plugin to run your serverless application locally. First, install the plugin:

```bash
npm install serverless-offline --save-dev
```

Then, add the plugin to your `serverless.yml` file:

```yaml
plugins:
  - serverless-offline
```

You can now start the local server with:

```bash
serverless offline
```

This command starts a local server that mimics the AWS API Gateway, allowing you to test your endpoints locally.

Step 11: Use Virtual Environments for Python Dependencies

For managing Python dependencies, it's a good practice to use a virtual environment. Create and activate a virtual environment in your project directory:

```bash
python -m venv venv
source venv/bin/activate  # On Windows use `venv\Scripts\activate`
```

Install any necessary dependencies:

```bash
pip install requests  # Example dependency
```

To ensure these dependencies are packaged with your function, include them in a `requirements.txt` file:

```bash
pip freeze > requirements.txt
```

Then, update your `serverless.yml` to use the `serverless-python-requirements` plugin:

```yaml
plugins:
  - serverless-python-requirements

custom:
  pythonRequirements:
    dockerizePip: true
```

Install the plugin:

```bash
npm install serverless-python-requirements --save-dev
```

Step 12: Deploying Updates

Whenever you make changes to your function or configuration, you can redeploy your application:

```bash
serverless deploy
```

This command updates the deployed resources and function code.

Step 13: Removing the Service

If you need to remove the deployed service from AWS, you can use:

```bash
serverless remove
```

This command removes all the resources created during deployment.

Setting up the Serverless Framework and configuring your local development environment for Python projects involves several steps, from installing the necessary tools to defining and deploying your serverless functions. By following this guide, you can streamline your serverless development workflow, enabling efficient local testing and seamless deployment. The Serverless Framework's extensibility and support for multiple cloud providers make it a powerful tool for building scalable, event-driven applications.

Understanding the Serverless Framework Project Structure: Configuration Files and Code Organization

The Serverless Framework simplifies the process of developing, deploying, and managing serverless applications across multiple cloud providers. Understanding the project structure, configuration files, and code organization is essential for efficiently leveraging the Serverless Framework. This article will delve into the key components of a Serverless Framework project, focusing on configuration files and best practices for organizing your code, particularly in Python.

Overview of the Serverless Framework Project Structure

When you create a new serverless project using the Serverless Framework, it generates a basic structure with several key files and directories. Here's an example structure for a typical Serverless Framework project:

```
my-serverless-app/
├── handler.py
├── serverless.yml
└── .gitignore
```

Each of these components plays a vital role in defining and managing your serverless application.

Key Components of the Project Structure

1. `serverless.yml`

The `serverless.yml` file is the heart of a Serverless Framework project. It is where you define your service configuration, including the functions, events, resources, and plugins your application will use. Here is a breakdown of a typical `serverless.yml` file:

```yaml
```

```
service: my-serverless-app

provider:
  name: aws
  runtime: python3.8
  region: us-east-1

functions:
  hello:
    handler: handler.hello
    events:
      - http:
          path: hello
          method: get

plugins:
  - serverless-python-requirements

custom:
  pythonRequirements:
    dockerizePip: true
```

Sections Explained:

- **Service**: The name of your service. This is usually the name of your project.

- **Provider**: Specifies the cloud provider and runtime environment. In this example, AWS and Python 3.8 are used.

- **Functions**: Defines the functions in your service. Each function has a handler and can have multiple events that trigger it.

- **Events**: Events are triggers for your functions, such as HTTP requests.

- **Plugins**: A list of plugins to extend the functionality of the Serverless Framework.

- **Custom**: Custom configurations for plugins and other custom settings.

2. `handler.py`

The `handler.py` file contains the implementation of your serverless functions. This is where you write the code for the Lambda functions defined in `serverless.yml`. Here's an example of a simple function:

```python
import json

def hello(event, context):
    body = {
        "message": "Hello, World!",
        "input": event
    }

    response = {
        "statusCode": 200,
        "body": json.dumps(body)
    }

    return response
```

This function is triggered by an HTTP GET request to the `/hello` endpoint, as defined in `serverless.yml`.

3. `.gitignore`

The `.gitignore` file specifies which files and directories should be ignored by version control systems like Git. This is important for excluding sensitive information and unnecessary files from your repository. A typical `.gitignore` for a Serverless Framework project might include:

```
# Byte-compiled / optimized / DLL files
__pycache__/
*.py[cod]
*$py.class

# C extensions
*.so

# Packages
*.egg
*.egg-info
dist
build
.eggs

# Serverless framework specific files
.serverless/
.env

# Virtual environments
venv/
```

```

## Organizing Your Code

As your serverless project grows, maintaining a well-organized codebase becomes crucial. Here are some best practices for organizing your Serverless Framework project:

**1. Separate Business Logic from Handlers**

To maintain clean and maintainable code, separate your business logic from the Lambda handlers. Create a `services` or `lib` directory to house your core application logic.

**Example directory structure:**

```
my-serverless-app/
├── handler.py
├── serverless.yml
├── .gitignore
└── services/
    └── my_service.py
```
```

In `handler.py`:

```python
from services.my_service import process_request
import json

def hello(event, context):
    result = process_request(event)
    response = {
        "statusCode": 200,
        "body": json.dumps(result)
    }
    return response
```

In `services/my_service.py`:

```python
def process_request(event):
    return {
        "message": "Hello, World!",
        "input": event
    }
```

2. Use Environment Variables

Storing sensitive data directly in your code is a bad practice. Instead, use environment variables to manage configuration settings and secrets. You can define environment variables in the `serverless.yml` file:

```yaml
provider:
  name: aws
  runtime: python3.8
  region: us-east-1
  environment:
    STAGE: ${opt:stage, 'dev'}
    DB_HOST: ${env:DB_HOST}
    DB_USER: ${env:DB_USER}
    DB_PASSWORD: ${env:DB_PASSWORD}
```

Load these variables in your Python code using the `os` module:

```python
import os

DB_HOST = os.environ['DB_HOST']
DB_USER = os.environ['DB_USER']
```

```
DB_PASSWORD = os.environ['DB_PASSWORD']
```

3. Managing Dependencies

For Python projects, it is best practice to use virtual environments to manage dependencies. You can use `venv` or `virtualenv` to create isolated environments for your project. Include a `requirements.txt` file to specify your dependencies.

Create a virtual environment:

```bash
python -m venv venv
source venv/bin/activate  # On Windows, use `venv\Scripts\activate`
```

Install dependencies and freeze them into `requirements.txt`:

```bash
pip install requests
pip freeze > requirements.txt
```

Include the `serverless-python-requirements` plugin in `serverless.yml` to package these dependencies:

```yaml
plugins:
  - serverless-python-requirements

custom:
  pythonRequirements:
    dockerizePip: true
```

4. Structuring the Project for Multiple Functions

If your project contains multiple Lambda functions, structure your project directories to logically group related functions. This approach keeps your code organized and manageable.

Example structure:

```
my-serverless-app/
├── functions/
│   ├── hello.py
```

```
│   ├── goodbye.py
│   └── utils.py
├── serverless.yml
└── .gitignore
```

In `serverless.yml`:

```yaml
functions:
  hello:
    handler: functions/hello.handler
    events:
      - http:
          path: hello
          method: get
  goodbye:
    handler: functions/goodbye.handler
    events:
      - http:
          path: goodbye
          method: post
```

Advanced Configuration

As your project grows, you may need to use advanced configurations in `serverless.yml`:

1. Custom Resources

You can define custom resources in `serverless.yml` to extend your serverless application with additional AWS services:

```yaml
resources:
  Resources:
    MyDynamoDBTable:
      Type: AWS::DynamoDB::Table
      Properties:
        TableName: MyTable
        AttributeDefinitions:
          - AttributeName: id
            AttributeType: S
        KeySchema:
          - AttributeName: id
            KeyType: HASH
        ProvisionedThroughput:
          ReadCapacityUnits: 1
          WriteCapacityUnits: 1
```

2. Conditional Resource Creation

You can use conditions to create resources based on deployment stages or other parameters:

```yaml
provider:
  name: aws
  runtime: python3.8
  stage: ${opt:stage, 'dev'}

custom:
  stages:
    dev:
      resources: true
    prod:
      resources: false

resources:
  Conditions:
    CreateResources: !Equals [ ${self:custom.stages.${self:provider.stage}.resources}, true ]
  Resources:
    MyDynamoDBTable:
```

```
    Condition: CreateResources
    Type: AWS::DynamoDB::Table
    Properties:
      TableName: MyTable
      AttributeDefinitions:
        - AttributeName: id
          AttributeType: S
      KeySchema:
        - AttributeName: id
          KeyType: HASH
      ProvisionedThroughput:
        ReadCapacityUnits: 1
        WriteCapacityUnits: 1
```

Understanding the Serverless Framework project structure and best practices for configuration and code organization is crucial for building scalable and maintainable serverless applications. By properly structuring your project, separating business logic, using environment variables, managing dependencies, and leveraging advanced configuration options, you can create robust serverless applications with ease.

The Serverless Framework provides a flexible and powerful toolset that simplifies serverless development, allowing you to focus on writing code and delivering value rather than managing infrastructure. With these guidelines, you can harness the full potential of serverless architecture for your Python projects.

Writing Your First Serverless Function with Python: A Hands-on Example

The Serverless Framework is a powerful tool for building and deploying serverless applications. In this hands-on example, we'll walk through writing your first serverless function using Python, deploying it to AWS Lambda, and testing it. This guide will help you get started with the Serverless Framework and understand its basic functionalities.

Prerequisites

Before we begin, make sure you have the following installed:

1. Node.js and npm: The Serverless Framework is a Node.js application. Download and install from nodejs.org.

2. Python: Ensure Python 3.8 or later is installed. Download from [python.org](https://www.python.org/downloads/).

3. AWS CLI: Install and configure the AWS CLI. Follow the instructions in the [AWS CLI User Guide](https://docs.aws.amazon.com/cli/latest/userguide/install-cliv2.html).

Step 1: Install the Serverless Framework

First, install the Serverless Framework globally using npm:

```bash
npm install -g serverless
```

Verify the installation:

```bash
serverless --version
```

Step 2: Set Up AWS Credentials

Configure your AWS CLI with your credentials:

```bash
aws configure
```

You'll need to enter your AWS Access Key ID, Secret Access Key, region, and output format.

Step 3: Create a New Serverless Project

Create a new Serverless project using the `aws-python3` template:

```bash
serverless create --template aws-python3 --path my-first-serverless-app
cd my-first-serverless-app
```

This command creates a directory named `my-first-serverless-app` with the following structure:

```
my-first-serverless-app/
├── handler.py
```

```
├── serverless.yml
└── .gitignore
```

Step 4: Write Your First Function

Open `handler.py` and replace its contents with the following code:

```python
import json

def hello(event, context):
    body = {
        "message": "Hello, World!",
        "input": event
    }

    response = {
        "statusCode": 200,
        "body": json.dumps(body)
    }

    return response
```

This simple function returns a JSON response with a "Hello, World!" message and the input event.

Step 5: Configure Your Serverless Service

Open `serverless.yml` and ensure it has the following configuration:

```yaml
service: my-first-serverless-app

provider:
  name: aws
  runtime: python3.8
  region: us-east-1

functions:
  hello:
    handler: handler.hello
    events:
      - http:
          path: hello
          method: get
```

This configuration file defines the service name, the provider (AWS), the runtime (Python 3.8), and a single function named `hello` that is triggered by an HTTP GET request to the `/hello` path.

Step 6: Deploy Your Function

Deploy your function to AWS Lambda using the following command:

```bash
serverless deploy
```

The deployment process will package your code, create the necessary AWS resources, and deploy your function. After deployment, you will see output similar to this:

```
Service Information
service: my-first-serverless-app
stage: dev
region: us-east-1
stack: my-first-serverless-app-dev
resources: 6
api keys:
```

      None
endpoints:
  GET - https://xxxxxxx.execute-api.us-east-1.amazonaws.com/dev/hello
functions:
  hello: my-first-serverless-app-dev-hello
layers:
  None
```

## Step 7: Test Your Deployed Function

To test your function, you can use `curl` or any API testing tool to send a GET request to the endpoint URL provided in the deployment output:

```bash
curl https://xxxxxxx.execute-api.us-east-1.amazonaws.com/dev/hello
```

You should receive a response similar to:

```json
{
  "message": "Hello, World!",

```
  "input": {
    // request details
  }
}
```

Step 8: Invoke Your Function Locally

For local development and testing, the Serverless Framework provides the ability to invoke functions locally. Run the following command to invoke the `hello` function locally:

```bash
serverless invoke local --function hello
```

This command runs your function locally and prints the output, which helps in quick testing and debugging.

Step 9: Use Environment Variables

Using environment variables to manage configuration settings and secrets is a good practice. Update your `serverless.yml` to include environment variables:

```yaml
```

```yaml
provider:
  name: aws
  runtime: python3.8
  region: us-east-1
  environment:
    STAGE: ${opt:stage, 'dev'}
    GREETING: "Hello, Serverless!"
```

Modify your function to use the `GREETING` environment variable:

```python
import json
import os

def hello(event, context):
    greeting = os.environ['GREETING']
    body = {
        "message": greeting,
        "input": event
    }

    response = {
        "statusCode": 200,
        "body": json.dumps(body)
```

```
    }

    return response
```

Deploy the updated function:

```bash
serverless deploy
```

Step 10: Organize Your Code

As your project grows, organizing your code into modules and packages improves maintainability. Create a directory structure like this:

```
my-first-serverless-app/
├── handler.py
├── serverless.yml
├── .gitignore
└── services/
    └── greeting_service.py
```

Move the business logic to a separate module:

```python
# services/greeting_service.py
def get_greeting():
    return "Hello, Modular World!"
```

Update `handler.py` to use this service:

```python
import json
from services.greeting_service import get_greeting

def hello(event, context):
    greeting = get_greeting()
    body = {
        "message": greeting,
        "input": event
    }

    response = {
        "statusCode": 200,
        "body": json.dumps(body)
    }
```

    return response
```

**Step 11: Manage Dependencies**

For Python projects, use a virtual environment to manage dependencies. Create and activate a virtual environment:

```bash
python -m venv venv
source venv/bin/activate  # On Windows, use `venv\Scripts\activate`
```

Install necessary packages and freeze the dependencies:

```bash
pip install requests
pip freeze > requirements.txt
```

Include the `serverless-python-requirements` plugin in your `serverless.yml`:

```yaml

```
plugins:
  - serverless-python-requirements

custom:
  pythonRequirements:
    dockerizePip: true
```

Install the plugin:

```bash
npm install serverless-python-requirements --save-dev
```

Deploy your service to ensure dependencies are included:

```bash
serverless deploy
```

Step 12: Use Serverless Offline for Local API Development

For extensive local development, use the `serverless-offline` plugin. Install the plugin:

```bash
npm install serverless-offline --save-dev
```

Add the plugin to your `serverless.yml`:

```yaml
plugins:
  - serverless-python-requirements
  - serverless-offline
```

Start the local server:

```bash
serverless offline
```

This command starts a local server that mimics the AWS API Gateway, allowing you to test your endpoints locally at `http://localhost:3000`.

Writing your first serverless function with Python using the Serverless Framework is a straightforward process that involves setting up your environment, writing and organizing your code, and deploying it to AWS Lambda. By following this hands-on example, you can quickly get up and running with serverless development.

The Serverless Framework's extensibility and support for multiple cloud providers make it a powerful tool for building scalable, event-driven applications. With this foundation, you can continue to explore more advanced features and best practices, such as integrating with other AWS services, optimizing performance, and enhancing security.

Chapter 4

Creating Powerful Serverless Functions: The Building Blocks of Your Applications

Defining Serverless Functions in Python: Understanding Handlers, Events, and Context

Serverless computing has transformed the way developers build and deploy applications. It eliminates the need for managing servers, allowing developers to focus solely on writing code. This article explores the key concepts involved in defining serverless functions in Python using the Serverless Framework, with a detailed look at handlers, events, and context.

Understanding Handlers

A handler is the entry point for a serverless function. It is responsible for processing the incoming request, executing the core logic, and returning a response. In the context of AWS Lambda, a handler is a specific Python function within your code.

Defining a Handler

To define a handler, you need to specify a function within a Python module. The `serverless.yml` configuration file maps the handler to an AWS Lambda function. Let's start with a basic example:

1. Project Structure:

```
my-serverless-app/
├── handler.py
└── serverless.yml
```

2. serverless.yml:

```yaml
service: my-serverless-app

provider:
  name: aws
  runtime: python3.8
  region: us-east-1

functions:
```

```
hello:
  handler: handler.hello
  events:
    - http:
        path: hello
        method: get
```

3. handler.py:

```python
import json

def hello(event, context):
    body = {
        "message": "Hello, World!",
        "input": event
    }
    response = {
```

```
        "statusCode": 200,

        "body": json.dumps(body)

    }

    return response
```

In this example, the `hello` function serves as the handler. The `serverless.yml` configuration maps the `hello` function to an HTTP GET request at the `/hello` endpoint.

Understanding Events

Events are the triggers that invoke your serverless functions. The Serverless Framework supports a variety of event sources, including HTTP requests via API Gateway, S3 bucket events, DynamoDB streams, scheduled events, and more. Each event source has its own configuration in the `serverless.yml` file.

HTTP Events

HTTP events are among the most common triggers. They are configured under the `events` section for each function. Here's an example:

```yaml
```

```
functions:
  createUser:
    handler: handler.create_user
    events:
      - http:
          path: user
          method: post
```

In this configuration, the `createUser` function is triggered by an HTTP POST request to the `/user` endpoint.

Understanding Context

The context object provides information about the invocation, function, and execution environment. It is automatically passed to the handler by AWS Lambda. The context object contains several properties and methods, including:

- **aws_request_id**: The unique identifier for the request.

- **log_group_name**: The name of the CloudWatch log group for the Lambda function.
- **log_stream_name**: The name of the CloudWatch log stream for the Lambda function.
- **function_name**: The name of the Lambda function.
- **memory_limit_in_mb**: The configured memory limit for the Lambda function.
- **get_remaining_time_in_millis()**: The number of milliseconds left before the execution times out.

Using the Context Object

Here's an example of how to use the context object in your handler:

```python
import json

def hello(event, context):
    body = {
        "message": "Hello, World!",
        "input": event,
        "request_id": context.aws_request_id,
        "function_name": context.function_name,
```

```
    "remaining_time_ms": 
context.get_remaining_time_in_millis()

  }

  response = {

    "statusCode": 200,

    "body": json.dumps(body)

  }

  return response
```
```

In this example, the response includes the AWS request ID, the function name, and the remaining execution time.

## Detailed Example: CRUD Operations with DynamoDB

Let's expand our example to include basic CRUD operations with DynamoDB. We will define multiple handlers, events, and use the context object.

### 1. Project Structure:

```

```
my-serverless-app/
├── handler.py
├── serverless.yml
└── requirements.txt
```

2. serverless.yml:

```yaml
service: my-serverless-app

provider:
  name: aws
  runtime: python3.8
  region: us-east-1
  environment:
    DYNAMODB_TABLE: ${self:service}-${opt:stage, self:provider.stage}

functions:
```

```
createUser:
  handler: handler.create_user
  events:
    - http:
        path: user
        method: post
getUser:
  handler: handler.get_user
  events:
    - http:
        path: user/{id}
        method: get
updateUser:
  handler: handler.update_user
  events:
    - http:
```

          path: user/{id}

          method: put

    deleteUser:

      handler: handler.delete_user

      events:

        - http:

            path: user/{id}

            method: delete

resources:

  Resources:

    UsersTable:

      Type: AWS::DynamoDB::Table

      Properties:

        TableName: ${self:provider.environment.DYNAMODB_TABLE}

        AttributeDefinitions:

```
      - AttributeName: id
        AttributeType: S
    KeySchema:
      - AttributeName: id
        KeyType: HASH
    ProvisionedThroughput:
      ReadCapacityUnits: 5
      WriteCapacityUnits: 5
```

3. handler.py:

```python
import json
import boto3
import os
from botocore.exceptions import ClientError

dynamodb = boto3.resource('dynamodb')
```

```python
table = dynamodb.Table(os.environ['DYNAMODB_TABLE'])

def create_user(event, context):
    data = json.loads(event['body'])
    if 'id' not in data or 'name' not in data:
        return {
            "statusCode": 400,
            "body": json.dumps({"error": "Invalid user data"})
        }
    item = {
        'id': data['id'],
        'name': data['name']
    }
    try:
        table.put_item(Item=item)
        return {
```

```python
            "statusCode": 200,
            "body": json.dumps(item)
        }
    except ClientError as e:
        return {
            "statusCode": 500,
            "body": json.dumps({"error": str(e)})
        }
def get_user(event, context):
    user_id = event['pathParameters']['id']
    try:
        result = table.get_item(Key={'id': user_id})
        if 'Item' in result:
            return {
                "statusCode": 200,
                "body": json.dumps(result['Item'])
```

```python
        }
    else:
        return {
            "statusCode": 404,
            "body": json.dumps({"error": "User not found"})
        }
except ClientError as e:
    return {
        "statusCode": 500,
        "body": json.dumps({"error": str(e)})
    }

def update_user(event, context):
    user_id = event['pathParameters']['id']
    data = json.loads(event['body'])
    if 'name' not in data:
```

```
    return {
        "statusCode": 400,
        "body": json.dumps({"error": "Invalid user data"})
    }
try:
    result = table.update_item(
        Key={'id': user_id},
        UpdateExpression='SET #name = :name',
        ExpressionAttributeNames={'#name': 'name'},
        ExpressionAttributeValues={':name': data['name']},
        ReturnValues='ALL_NEW'
    )
    return {
        "statusCode": 200,
        "body": json.dumps(result['Attributes'])
```

```python
    }
    except ClientError as e:
        return {
            "statusCode": 500,
            "body": json.dumps({"error": str(e)})
        }

def delete_user(event, context):
    user_id = event['pathParameters']['id']
    try:
        table.delete_item(Key={'id': user_id})
        return {
            "statusCode": 200,
            "body": json.dumps({"message": "User deleted"})
        }
    except ClientError as e:
```

```
return {
    "statusCode": 500,
    "body": json.dumps({"error": str(e)})
}
```

4. requirements.txt:

```
boto3
```

Explanation

1. Handlers: We defined four handlers: `create_user`, `get_user`, `update_user`, and `delete_user`. Each function processes the corresponding CRUD operation for DynamoDB.

2. Events: Each handler is triggered by an HTTP event. The path and method are specified in the `serverless.yml` file.

3. Context: The context object is passed to each handler, but in this example, it's not explicitly used. It can be used for logging, tracking request IDs, and more.

4. Environment Variables: The DynamoDB table name is set using an environment variable, ensuring it can be easily modified without changing the code.

Testing and Deployment

Deploy the service:

```bash
serverless deploy
```

Test the endpoints using `curl` or an API client like Postman. For example:

1. Create User:

```bash
curl -X POST https://xxxxxxx.execute-api.us-east-1.amazonaws.com/dev/user -d '{"id": "1", "name": "John Doe"}'
```

2. Get User:

```bash
curl https://xxxxxxx.execute-api.us-east-1.amazonaws.com/dev/user/1
```

3. Update User:

```bash
curl -X PUT https://xxxxxxx.execute-api.us-east-1.amazonaws.com/dev/user/1 -d '{"name": "Jane Doe"}'
```

4. Delete User:

```bash
curl -X DELETE https://xxxxxxx.execute-api.us-east-1.amazonaws.com/dev/user/1
```

In this detailed hands-on example, we have covered how to define serverless functions using Python with the Serverless Framework. We explored the key components such as handlers, events, and the context object.

Additionally, we demonstrated how to set up and configure a project, deploy it to AWS Lambda, and interact with it using HTTP requests. By following these steps, you can build scalable and efficient serverless applications with ease.

Let's summarize the key points:

1. Handlers: The entry point for serverless functions. They process incoming requests and return responses.

2. Events: Triggers that invoke your serverless functions. These can be HTTP requests, S3 events, DynamoDB streams, etc.

3. Context: Provides information about the invocation, function, and execution environment. Useful for logging and tracking execution details.

4. Configuration: The `serverless.yml` file is the central configuration file where you define your functions, events, resources, and environment variables.

5. Dependency Management: Use virtual environments and requirements files to manage dependencies and ensure they are packaged correctly with your deployment.

By mastering these concepts and the Serverless Framework, you can focus on writing business logic without worrying about server management, scaling, and infrastructure. This approach not only saves time and reduces operational complexity but also enables rapid development and deployment of cloud-native applications.

Feel free to extend this example by integrating other AWS services, adding more complex business logic, or implementing additional features like authentication and logging. The Serverless Framework's extensive plugin ecosystem and robust support for various cloud providers make it a versatile choice for any serverless project. Happy coding!

Handling Different Types of Events: HTTP Requests, Queues, and More

In the realm of serverless computing, handling various types of events such as HTTP requests, message queues, and other triggers is essential for creating scalable and efficient applications. The Serverless Framework, coupled with Python, provides a robust environment for developing, deploying, and managing these event-driven architectures. This guide will explore how to handle different types of events using the Serverless Framework with Python, including practical examples and code snippets.

Prerequisites

Before diving into the implementation, ensure you have the following prerequisites:

- Node.js and npm installed.

- Serverless Framework installed globally via npm (`npm install -g serverless`).

- AWS account for deploying serverless functions.

- Basic knowledge of Python and serverless concepts.

Setting Up a Serverless Python Project

Start by creating a new Serverless project:

```bash
serverless create --template aws-python3 --path my-serverless-app
cd my-serverless-app
```

This command creates a new Serverless project with a basic structure. Open the `serverless.yml` file, which is the configuration file for defining your serverless services and functions.

Handling HTTP Requests

HTTP requests are one of the most common events in serverless applications. The Serverless Framework makes it straightforward to define HTTP endpoints and link them to Lambda functions.

Example: Handling an HTTP GET Request

1. Define the function and HTTP endpoint in `serverless.yml`:

```yaml
service: my-serverless-app
```

```
provider:
  name: aws
  runtime: python3.8
  region: us-east-1

functions:
  getUser:
    handler: handler.get_user
    events:
      - http:
          path: users/{id}
          method: get
          cors: true
```

2. Implement the `get_user` function in `handler.py`:

```python
import json

def get_user(event, context):
    user_id = event['pathParameters']['id']

    # Simulate fetching user data from a database
    user_data = {
        "id": user_id,
```

```
    "name": "John Doe",
    "email": "john.doe@example.com"
}

response = {
    "statusCode": 200,
    "body": json.dumps(user_data)
}

return response
```

Deploy the function using:

```bash
serverless deploy
```

After deployment, an endpoint URL will be provided. You can test the function using tools like `curl` or Postman.

```bash
curl https://<api_id>.execute-api.<region>.amazonaws.com/dev/users/123
```

Handling Message Queues

Message queues, such as Amazon SQS, are vital for decoupling services and managing asynchronous workflows. Serverless functions can be triggered by new messages arriving in an SQS queue.

Example: Handling an SQS Message

1. Define the function and SQS event in `serverless.yml`:

```yaml
functions:
  processQueueMessage:
    handler: handler.process_queue_message
    events:
      - sqs:
          arn:
            Fn::GetAtt:
              - MyQueue
              - Arn
resources:
  Resources:
    MyQueue:
      Type: "AWS::SQS::Queue"
```

```
    Properties:
      QueueName: "MyQueue"
```

2. Implement the `process_queue_message` function in `handler.py`:

```python
import json

def process_queue_message(event, context):
    for record in event['Records']:
        message_body = record['body']
        print(f"Processing message: {message_body}")

        # Process the message (e.g., store in database, trigger another process)

    return {
        "statusCode": 200,
        "body": json.dumps({"message": "Messages processed"})
    }
```

Deploy the function and create the SQS queue using:

```bash
serverless deploy
```

To send a test message to the SQS queue, use the AWS CLI:

```bash
aws sqs send-message --queue-url https://sqs.<region>.amazonaws.com/<account-id>/MyQueue --message-body "Hello, Serverless!"
```

Handling Scheduled Events

Scheduled events (cron jobs) are useful for periodic tasks such as cleaning up databases or generating reports.

Example: Handling a Scheduled Event

1. Define the function and scheduled event in `serverless.yml`:

```yaml
functions:
```

```
scheduledTask:
  handler: handler.scheduled_task
  events:
    - schedule:
        rate: rate(1 hour)
        enabled: true
```

2. Implement the `scheduled_task` function in `handler.py`:

```python
import json
import datetime

def scheduled_task(event, context):
    current_time = datetime.datetime.now().isoformat()
    print(f"Scheduled task running at {current_time}")

    # Perform the scheduled task (e.g., cleanup, generate report)

    return {
        "statusCode": 200,
        "body": json.dumps({"message": "Scheduled task executed"})
```

```
    }
```

Deploy the function:

```bash
serverless deploy
```

The function will automatically trigger based on the specified schedule (e.g., every hour).

Handling DynamoDB Streams

DynamoDB Streams capture changes to items in a DynamoDB table, allowing serverless functions to react to database updates in real-time.

Example: Handling DynamoDB Stream Events

1. Define the function and DynamoDB stream event in `serverless.yml`:

```yaml
functions:
  processDynamoDBStream:
```

```
      handler: handler.process_dynamodb_stream
      events:
        - stream:
            type: dynamodb
            arn:
              Fn::GetAtt:
                - MyDynamoDBTable
                - StreamArn
resources:
  Resources:
    MyDynamoDBTable:
      Type: "AWS::DynamoDB::Table"
      Properties:
        TableName: "MyDynamoDBTable"
        AttributeDefinitions:
          - AttributeName: id
            AttributeType: S
        KeySchema:
          - AttributeName: id
            KeyType: HASH
        StreamSpecification:
          StreamViewType: NEW_IMAGE
        ProvisionedThroughput:
          ReadCapacityUnits: 5
          WriteCapacityUnits: 5
```

2. Implement the `process_dynamodb_stream` function in `handler.py`:

```python
import json

def process_dynamodb_stream(event, context):
    for record in event['Records']:
        if record['eventName'] == 'INSERT':
            new_image = record['dynamodb']['NewImage']
            print(f"New item added: {json.dumps(new_image)}")

            # Process the new item (e.g., update another table, trigger a notification)

    return {
        "statusCode": 200,
        "body": json.dumps({"message": "DynamoDB stream processed"})
    }
```

Deploy the function and create the DynamoDB table with:

```bash
serverless deploy
```

Now, any new item inserted into the DynamoDB table will trigger the `process_dynamodb_stream` function.

Handling different types of events such as HTTP requests, message queues, scheduled tasks, and DynamoDB streams is fundamental in building robust serverless applications. The Serverless Framework, along with Python, provides an efficient way to define and manage these event-driven functions. By following the examples provided, you can extend these concepts to fit your specific application needs, ensuring scalability and responsiveness in your serverless architecture.

Advanced Function Design: Asynchronous Programming, Caching Strategies, and Error Handling

In advanced serverless application development, optimizing for performance and resilience is crucial. This involves using asynchronous programming to handle concurrent tasks efficiently, implementing caching strategies to reduce latency and load, and employing robust error handling to ensure application reliability. This guide explores these advanced concepts in the context of the Serverless Framework and Python, providing practical examples and code snippets.

Asynchronous Programming

Asynchronous programming allows functions to run concurrently, improving performance, especially in I/O-bound applications. Python's `asyncio` library is a powerful tool for implementing asynchronous code in serverless functions.

Example: Asynchronous HTTP Requests

1. Update `serverless.yml` to include a new function:

```yaml
functions:
  asyncHttpRequest:
    handler: handler.async_http_request
    events:
      - http:
          path: async-request
          method: get
```

```
      cors: true
```

2. Implement the `async_http_request` function in `handler.py` using `asyncio` and `aiohttp`:

```python
import json
import asyncio
import aiohttp

async def fetch_url(session, url):
    async with session.get(url) as response:
        return await response.text()

async def async_http_request(event, context):
    urls = [
        "https://api.example.com/data1",
        "https://api.example.com/data2",
        "https://api.example.com/data3"
    ]

    async with aiohttp.ClientSession() as session:
        tasks = [fetch_url(session, url) for url in urls]
        responses = await asyncio.gather(*tasks)
```

```
    return {
        "statusCode": 200,
        "body": json.dumps({"responses": responses})
    }
```

Deploy the function:

```bash
serverless deploy
```

The `async_http_request` function makes multiple HTTP requests concurrently, significantly reducing the total execution time compared to sequential requests.

Caching Strategies

Caching can greatly enhance performance by reducing the number of redundant computations and external API calls. AWS offers several caching solutions, such as AWS Lambda's built-in cache and AWS ElastiCache.

Example: Caching with AWS Lambda Built-in Cache

Lambda's execution environment can retain state between invocations, allowing for simple in-memory caching.

1. Define a function in `serverless.yml`:

```yaml
functions:
  cachedFunction:
    handler: handler.cached_function
    events:
      - http:
          path: cached-endpoint
          method: get
          cors: true
```

2. Implement the `cached_function` in `handler.py`:

```python
import json
import time

# In-memory cache
cache = {}
```

```python
def expensive_computation():
    time.sleep(2)  # Simulate a long computation
    return {"data": "Computed result"}

def cached_function(event, context):
    cache_key = "expensive_result"

    if cache_key in cache:
        result = cache[cache_key]
    else:
        result = expensive_computation()
        cache[cache_key] = result

    return {
        "statusCode": 200,
        "body": json.dumps(result)
    }
```

Deploy the function:

```bash
serverless deploy
```

This example shows a basic in-memory cache that retains data between Lambda invocations, reducing the need for repetitive, expensive computations.

Example: Caching with AWS ElastiCache

For more advanced caching, AWS ElastiCache with Redis can be used to manage state across different Lambda instances.

1. First, set up an ElastiCache cluster through the AWS Management Console.

2. Define a function in `serverless.yml`:

```yaml
functions:
  redisCacheFunction:
    handler: handler.redis_cache_function
    events:
      - http:
          path: redis-cached-endpoint
          method: get
          cors: true
```

3. Install the `redis` library:

```bash
pip install redis
```

4. Implement the `redis_cache_function` in `handler.py`:

```python
import json
import time
import redis

# Connect to Redis (update with your ElastiCache endpoint)
redis_client = redis.StrictRedis(host='your-redis-endpoint', port=6379, db=0)

def expensive_computation():
    time.sleep(2)  # Simulate a long computation
    return {"data": "Computed result"}

def redis_cache_function(event, context):
    cache_key = "expensive_result"

    cached_result = redis_client.get(cache_key)
```

```python
    if cached_result:
        result = json.loads(cached_result)
    else:
        result = expensive_computation()
        redis_client.set(cache_key, json.dumps(result))

    return {
        "statusCode": 200,
        "body": json.dumps(result)
    }
```

Deploy the function:

```bash
serverless deploy
```

By using ElastiCache, you can manage a centralized cache that multiple Lambda instances can access, providing a more scalable caching solution.

Error Handling

Proper error handling ensures that your application can gracefully handle failures and provide meaningful responses to clients. This involves catching exceptions, logging errors, and implementing retry mechanisms.

Example: Basic Error Handling

1. Define a function in `serverless.yml`:

```yaml
functions:
  errorHandlingFunction:
    handler: handler.error_handling_function
    events:
      - http:
          path: error-endpoint
          method: get
          cors: true
```

2. Implement the `error_handling_function` in `handler.py`:

```python
import json

def error_handling_function(event, context):
    try:
```

```
        # Simulate an operation that might fail
        result = 1 / 0
        return {
            "statusCode": 200,
            "body": json.dumps({"result": result})
        }
    except ZeroDivisionError as e:
        return {
            "statusCode": 500,
            "body": json.dumps({"error": "Division by zero occurred"})
        }
    except Exception as e:
        return {
            "statusCode": 500,
            "body": json.dumps({"error": "An unexpected error occurred", "message": str(e)})
        }
```

Deploy the function:

```bash
serverless deploy
```

This function demonstrates basic error handling by catching exceptions and returning appropriate error messages.

Example: Advanced Error Handling with Retries

For transient errors, implementing retries can help ensure that temporary issues do not cause permanent failures.

1. Define a function with retry configuration in `serverless.yml`:

```yaml
functions:
  retryHandlingFunction:
    handler: handler.retry_handling_function
    events:
      - http:
          path: retry-endpoint
          method: get
          cors: true
    maximumRetryAttempts: 2
    backoffRate: 2.0
```

2. Implement the `retry_handling_function` in `handler.py`:

```python
import json
import random

def retry_handling_function(event, context):
    try:
        # Simulate an operation that might fail
        if random.choice([True, False]):
            raise ValueError("Simulated transient error")
        return {
            "statusCode": 200,
            "body": json.dumps({"message": "Success"})
        }
    except ValueError as e:
        print(f"Retryable error occurred: {e}")
        raise e  # Re-throw exception to trigger retry
    except Exception as e:
        return {
            "statusCode": 500,
            "body": json.dumps({"error": "An unexpected error occurred", "message": str(e)})
        }
```

Deploy the function:

```bash
serverless deploy
```

This example shows how to configure retries for a function using the Serverless Framework. The `maximumRetryAttempts` and `backoffRate` parameters control the retry behavior.

Example: Error Logging with AWS CloudWatch

Logging errors is essential for diagnosing issues. AWS CloudWatch provides a centralized service for collecting and analyzing log data.

1. Define a function in `serverless.yml`:

```yaml
functions:
  loggingFunction:
    handler: handler.logging_function
    events:
      - http:
```

```
      path: logging-endpoint
      method: get
      cors: true
```

2. Implement the `logging_function` in `handler.py`:

```python
import json
import logging

logger = logging.getLogger()
logger.setLevel(logging.INFO)

def logging_function(event, context):
    try:
        # Simulate an operation that might fail
        result = 1 / 0
        return {
            "statusCode": 200,
            "body": json.dumps({"result": result})
        }
    except ZeroDivisionError as e:
        logger.error("Division by zero error", exc_info=True)
        return {
```

```
        "statusCode": 500,
        "body": json.dumps({"error": "Division by zero occurred"})
    }
    except Exception as e:
        logger.error("An unexpected error occurred", exc_info=True)
        return {
            "statusCode": 500,
            "body": json.dumps({"error": "An unexpected error occurred", "message": str(e)})
        }
```

Deploy the function:

```bash
serverless deploy
```

This function logs errors to CloudWatch, making it easier to monitor and debug issues in your serverless application.

Advanced function design in serverless applications involves leveraging asynchronous programming, implementing effective caching strategies, and ensuring robust error handling. By adopting these techniques, you can create more performant, scalable, and resilient applications. The Serverless Framework, combined with Python, provides a powerful platform for developing these advanced features. By following the examples provided, you can enhance your serverless functions to handle complex real-world scenarios efficiently and reliably.

Chapter 5

Understanding Event Sources and Triggers for Your Functions: APIs, Queues, and More

In the world of cloud computing, particularly in the context of serverless architecture, understanding event sources and triggers is crucial for designing and deploying efficient applications. Serverless functions, such as those provided by AWS Lambda, Azure Functions, or Google Cloud Functions, rely on various event sources to execute. These event sources can range from HTTP requests via APIs to messages in a queue. In this article, we'll explore different event sources and triggers, and how to leverage them using the Python Serverless framework.

Overview of Serverless Framework

The Serverless Framework is a popular open-source tool that simplifies the deployment of serverless applications across different cloud providers. It allows developers to define functions, their triggers, and resources in a single configuration file (`serverless.yml`). This framework abstracts away much of the complexity involved in deploying serverless applications, enabling developers to focus on writing code.

Event Sources and Triggers

Event sources are the origins of events that trigger the execution of serverless functions. Each cloud provider offers a variety of event sources, such as:

- HTTP requests via APIs

- Message queues

- File uploads to cloud storage

- Scheduled events (cron jobs)

- Database changes

- Email messages

Let's delve into some common event sources and see how to configure them using the Serverless framework with Python.

HTTP Requests via APIs

One of the most common use cases for serverless functions is responding to HTTP requests. This is typically achieved using API Gateway (AWS), HTTP Triggers (Azure), or HTTP Functions (Google Cloud).

Here's an example of how to set up an AWS Lambda function triggered by an HTTP request using the Serverless framework.

`serverless.yml`

```yaml
service: my-http-service

provider:
  name: aws
  runtime: python3.8

functions:
  hello:
    handler: handler.hello
    events:
      - http:
          path: hello
          method: get
```

```

`handler.py`

```python
def hello(event, context):
    return {
        'statusCode': 200,
        'body': 'Hello, world!'
    }
```

In this configuration:

- `provider` specifies AWS as the cloud provider and Python 3.8 as the runtime.

- `functions` defines a function named `hello` that uses `handler.hello` as the entry point.

- `events` specifies that this function is triggered by an HTTP GET request to the `/hello` path.

Message Queues
```

Another common trigger for serverless functions is a message queue. AWS provides SQS (Simple Queue Service), while Azure offers Service Bus and Google Cloud has Pub/Sub.

Here's how to configure an AWS Lambda function to be triggered by messages in an SQS queue.

`serverless.yml`

```yaml
service: my-queue-service

provider:
  name: aws
  runtime: python3.8

functions:
  processQueue:
    handler: handler.process_queue
    events:
      - sqs:
          arn:
            Fn::GetAtt:
              - MyQueue
              - Arn
```

```
resources:
  Resources:
    MyQueue:
      Type: AWS::SQS::Queue
      Properties:
        QueueName: MyQueue
```

`handler.py`

```python
def process_queue(event, context):
    for record in event['Records']:
        print(f"Processing message: {record['body']}")
```

In this configuration:

- The function `processQueue` is triggered by messages in the `MyQueue` SQS queue.

- `resources` block is used to create the SQS queue as part of the deployment.

File Uploads to Cloud Storage

Serverless functions can also be triggered by file uploads to cloud storage services like S3 (AWS), Blob Storage (Azure), or Cloud Storage (Google Cloud).

Here's an example of an AWS Lambda function triggered by an S3 file upload.

`serverless.yml`

```yaml
service: my-storage-service

provider:
  name: aws
  runtime: python3.8

functions:
  processUpload:
    handler: handler.process_upload
    events:
      - s3:
          bucket: my-upload-bucket
          event: s3:ObjectCreated:*
```

`handler.py`

```python
def process_upload(event, context):
    for record in event['Records']:
        bucket = record['s3']['bucket']['name']
        key = record['s3']['object']['key']
        print(f"New file uploaded: {bucket}/{key}")
```

In this configuration:

- The function `processUpload` is triggered by any object creation event in the `my-upload-bucket` S3 bucket.

Scheduled Events

Scheduled events (cron jobs) are useful for periodic tasks such as cleanup operations, data processing, or sending notifications. AWS uses CloudWatch Events, Azure uses Timer Triggers, and Google Cloud uses Cloud Scheduler.

Here's an example of an AWS Lambda function triggered by a scheduled event.

`serverless.yml`

```yaml
service: my-scheduled-service

provider:
  name: aws
  runtime: python3.8

functions:
  scheduledTask:
    handler: handler.scheduled_task
    events:
      - schedule:
          rate: rate(1 hour)
```

`handler.py`

```python
def scheduled_task(event, context):
    print("Scheduled task executed")
```

In this configuration:

- The function `scheduledTask` is triggered every hour by a CloudWatch event rule.

Database Changes

Database changes can trigger serverless functions to perform operations such as caching, notifications, or further processing. AWS provides DynamoDB Streams, Azure uses Cosmos DB Change Feed, and Google Cloud has Firestore triggers.

Here's how to configure an AWS Lambda function to be triggered by changes in a DynamoDB table.

`serverless.yml`

```yaml
service: my-database-service

provider:
  name: aws
  runtime: python3.8

functions:
  processDynamoDBChanges:
```

```yaml
    handler: handler.process_dynamodb_changes
    events:
      - stream:
          type: dynamodb
          arn:
            Fn::GetAtt:
              - MyDynamoDBTable
              - StreamArn

resources:
  Resources:
    MyDynamoDBTable:
      Type: AWS::DynamoDB::Table
      Properties:
        TableName: MyTable
        AttributeDefinitions:
          - AttributeName: id
            AttributeType: S
        KeySchema:
          - AttributeName: id
            KeyType: HASH
        StreamSpecification:
          StreamViewType: NEW_IMAGE
        ProvisionedThroughput:
          ReadCapacityUnits: 1
          WriteCapacityUnits: 1
```

```

`handler.py`

```python
def process_dynamodb_changes(event, context):
    for record in event['Records']:
        print(f"Processing record: {record['dynamodb']}")
```

In this configuration:

- The function `processDynamoDBChanges` is triggered by changes in the `MyTable` DynamoDB table.

Email Messages

Email services like Amazon SES can also be used to trigger serverless functions. This can be useful for processing inbound emails, spam filtering, or automating responses.

Here's how to configure an AWS Lambda function to be triggered by an SES email receipt.
```

`serverless.yml`

```yaml
service: my-email-service

provider:
  name: aws
  runtime: python3.8

functions:
  processEmail:
    handler: handler.process_email
    events:
      - ses:
          rule: MySESRuleset
```

`handler.py`

```python
def process_email(event, context):
    for record in event['Records']:
        print(f"Processing email: {record['ses']['mail']['messageId']}")
```

In this configuration:

- The function `processEmail` is triggered by an SES email receipt rule named `MySESRuleset`.

Understanding the various event sources and triggers available in serverless architecture is key to building responsive and efficient applications. By leveraging the Serverless Framework, you can easily configure and deploy functions that respond to HTTP requests, process messages from queues, handle file uploads, execute scheduled tasks, react to database changes, and even process emails.

The examples provided in this article demonstrate how to configure these event sources using `serverless.yml` and Python handlers. Mastering these concepts will enable you to harness the full power of serverless computing, creating applications that are both scalable and cost-effective.

Building Event-Driven Workflows: Chaining Functions, Handling Complex Logic, and Fan-Out Patterns

Event-driven workflows in serverless architectures enable developers to build highly scalable and resilient applications. These workflows can chain functions, handle complex logic, and implement fan-out patterns to efficiently manage tasks. The Serverless Framework, combined with Python, offers a robust way to build these workflows across various cloud providers. This article explores how to build event-driven workflows by chaining functions, managing complex logic, and utilizing fan-out patterns.

Chaining Functions

Chaining functions allows you to execute a sequence of operations where each function triggers the next. This is useful for processes that require multiple steps, such as processing a file upload and then updating a database.

AWS Step Functions

AWS Step Functions provide a way to chain functions together using a state machine. Here's an example of a simple workflow using AWS Step Functions with the Serverless Framework.

`serverless.yml`

```yaml
service: my-chained-service

provider:
  name: aws
  runtime: python3.8
  iamRoleStatements:
    - Effect: "Allow"
      Action:
        - "states:StartExecution"
      Resource: "*"

functions:
  firstFunction:
    handler: handler.first_function
  secondFunction:
    handler: handler.second_function

stepFunctions:
  stateMachines:
    myStateMachine:
```

```
  definition:
    Comment: "A simple example of chaining functions"
    StartAt: FirstFunction
    States:
      FirstFunction:
        Type: Task
        Resource: arn:aws:lambda:#{AWS::Region}:#{AWS::AccountId}:function:${self:service}-${opt:stage, self:provider.stage}-firstFunction
        Next: SecondFunction
      SecondFunction:
        Type: Task
        Resource: arn:aws:lambda:#{AWS::Region}:#{AWS::AccountId}:function:${self:service}-${opt:stage, self:provider.stage}-secondFunction
        End: true
```

`handler.py`

```python
def first_function(event, context):
    print("First function executed")
```

```
    return {"message": "First function completed"}

def second_function(event, context):
    print("Second function executed")
    return {"message": "Second function completed"}
```

In this configuration:

- Two functions, `firstFunction` and `secondFunction`, are defined.

- An AWS Step Function state machine is configured to chain these functions.

When the state machine is triggered, `firstFunction` executed and, upon completion, triggers `secondFunction`.

Handling Complex Logic

Handling complex logic often involves conditional branching and retries. AWS Step Functions support these features, allowing you to manage sophisticated workflows.

Conditional Branching

Let's extend our previous example to include conditional branching based on the output of the first function.

`serverless.yml`

```yaml
service: my-complex-logic-service

provider:
  name: aws
  runtime: python3.8

functions:
  firstFunction:
    handler: handler.first_function
  secondFunction:
    handler: handler.second_function
  thirdFunction:
    handler: handler.third_function

stepFunctions:
  stateMachines:
    myComplexStateMachine:
      definition:
```

```yaml
Comment: "A workflow with complex logic"
StartAt: FirstFunction
States:
  FirstFunction:
    Type: Task
    Resource: arn:aws:lambda:#{AWS::Region}:#{AWS::AccountId}:function:${self:service}-${opt:stage, self:provider.stage}-firstFunction
    Next: ChoiceState
  ChoiceState:
    Type: Choice
    Choices:
      - Variable: "$.message"
        StringEquals: "First function completed"
        Next: SecondFunction
    Default: ThirdFunction
  SecondFunction:
    Type: Task
    Resource: arn:aws:lambda:#{AWS::Region}:#{AWS::AccountId}:function:${self:service}-${opt:stage, self:provider.stage}-secondFunction
    End: true
  ThirdFunction:
    Type: Task
```

          Resource:
arn:aws:lambda:#{AWS::Region}:#{AWS::AccountId}:function:${self:service}-${opt:stage, self:provider.stage}-thirdFunction
          End: true
```

`handler.py`

```python
def first_function(event, context):
    print("First function executed")
    return {"message": "First function completed"}

def second_function(event, context):
    print("Second function executed")
    return {"message": "Second function completed"}

def third_function(event, context):
    print("Third function executed")
    return {"message": "Third function completed"}
```

In this configuration:
```

- `ChoiceState` is introduced to handle conditional logic.

- Depending on the output of `firstFunction`, either `secondFunction` or `thirdFunction` is triggered.

Retry Logic

To handle transient errors, you can configure retries in AWS Step Functions.

`serverless.yml`

```yaml
service: my-retry-service

provider:
  name: aws
  runtime: python3.8

functions:
  firstFunction:
    handler: handler.first_function
  secondFunction:
    handler: handler.second_function
```

```yaml
stepFunctions:
  stateMachines:
    myRetryStateMachine:
      definition:
        Comment: "A workflow with retry logic"
        StartAt: FirstFunction
        States:
          FirstFunction:
            Type: Task
            Resource: arn:aws:lambda:#{AWS::Region}:#{AWS::AccountId}:function:${self:service}-${opt:stage, self:provider.stage}-firstFunction
            Retry:
              - ErrorEquals:
                  - "Lambda.ServiceException"
                  - "Lambda.AWSLambdaException"
                  - "Lambda.SdkClientException"
                IntervalSeconds: 2
                MaxAttempts: 3
                BackoffRate: 2.0
            Next: SecondFunction
          SecondFunction:
            Type: Task
            Resource: arn:aws:lambda:#{AWS::Region}:#{AWS::AccountId}:
```

```
function:${self:service}-${opt:stage,
self:provider.stage}-secondFunction
        End: true
```

In this configuration:

- The `Retry` field specifies how to retry the `firstFunction` if certain errors occur.

Fan-Out Patterns

Fan-out patterns allow you to trigger multiple functions concurrently from a single event. This is useful for tasks that can be parallelized, such as processing different parts of a dataset.

Using SNS for Fan-Out

AWS SNS (Simple Notification Service) can be used to implement fan-out patterns. You publish a message to an SNS topic, which triggers multiple Lambda functions.

`serverless.yml`

```yaml
```

```
service: my-fanout-service

provider:
  name: aws
  runtime: python3.8

functions:
  publisher:
    handler: handler.publisher
  consumerOne:
    handler: handler.consumer_one
    events:
      - sns: myTopic
  consumerTwo:
    handler: handler.consumer_two
    events:
      - sns: myTopic

resources:
  Resources:
    myTopic:
      Type: AWS::SNS::Topic
      Properties:
        TopicName: myTopic
```

`handler.py`

```python
import json
import boto3

sns_client = boto3.client('sns')

def publisher(event, context):
    message = {"text": "Hello from publisher"}
    sns_client.publish(
        TopicArn='arn:aws:sns:REGION:ACCOUNT_ID:myTopic',
        Message=json.dumps({'default': json.dumps(message)}),
        MessageStructure='json'
    )
    return {"statusCode": 200, "body": "Message published"}

def consumer_one(event, context):
    print("Consumer One received message: ", event['Records'][0]['Sns']['Message'])

def consumer_two(event, context):
```

```
    print("Consumer Two received message: ",
event['Records'][0]['Sns']['Message'])
```

In this configuration:

- `publisher` function publishes a message to the SNS topic `myTopic`.

- `consumerOne` and `consumerTwo` functions are triggered by messages to the `myTopic` SNS topic.

Building event-driven workflows in a serverless architecture involves chaining functions, handling complex logic, and implementing fan-out patterns. The Serverless Framework, combined with Python, provides a powerful and flexible way to define and deploy these workflows.

By chaining functions using AWS Step Functions, you can create sequences of operations with conditional branching and retry logic to handle complex workflows. Fan-out patterns using AWS SNS allow you to trigger multiple functions concurrently, enabling parallel processing and improving the efficiency of your applications.

Understanding and mastering these concepts will empower you to build scalable, resilient, and efficient serverless applications that can handle a wide variety of tasks and workflows.

Implementing Message Queues with SQS for Asynchronous Processing and Decoupling Functions

Message queues are a fundamental building block in modern software architectures, providing a mechanism for decoupling and asynchronously processing tasks. Amazon Simple Queue Service (SQS) is a fully managed message queuing service that enables you to decouple and scale microservices, distributed systems, and serverless applications. In this article, we will explore how to implement message queues with SQS for asynchronous processing and decoupling functions using the Serverless Framework and Python.

Benefits of Message Queues

1. Decoupling: Message queues allow you to decouple components of your application, making it easier to manage and scale each component independently.

2. Asynchronous Processing: Tasks can be processed asynchronously, improving the responsiveness and throughput of your application.

3. Scalability: Message queues can buffer requests and handle spikes in traffic, ensuring that your application remains responsive even under heavy load.

4. Fault Tolerance: By decoupling components, message queues can improve fault tolerance, allowing parts of your system to fail without affecting the entire application.

Overview of SQS

Amazon SQS offers two types of message queues:

- **Standard Queues:** Provide at-least-once delivery, best-effort ordering, and high throughput.

- **FIFO Queues:** Provide exactly-once processing and guaranteed message ordering, which is essential for applications that require strict order of operations.

Setting Up the Serverless Framework

Before we dive into the code, make sure you have the Serverless Framework installed and configured. You can install it globally using npm:

```bash
npm install -g serverless
```

Ensure you have AWS credentials configured on your local machine to deploy resources.

Creating an SQS Queue with the Serverless Framework

Let's start by defining an SQS queue in our `serverless.yml` configuration file and setting up a Lambda function that will process messages from this queue.

`serverless.yml`

```yaml
service: sqs-queue-service

provider:
  name: aws
  runtime: python3.8
  iamRoleStatements:
    - Effect: "Allow"
      Action:
        - "sqs:SendMessage"
        - "sqs:ReceiveMessage"
        - "sqs:DeleteMessage"
        - "sqs:GetQueueAttributes"
      Resource: "*"

functions:
  producer:
    handler: handler.producer
  consumer:
    handler: handler.consumer
    events:
      - sqs:
          arn:
            Fn::GetAtt:
```

```
      - MyQueue
      - Arn

resources:
  Resources:
    MyQueue:
      Type: AWS::SQS::Queue
      Properties:
        QueueName: MyQueue
        VisibilityTimeout: 60
```

In this configuration:

- We define two functions: `producer` and `consumer`.

- The `producer` function will send messages to the SQS queue.

- The `consumer` function will process messages from the SQS queue.

- We create an SQS queue named `MyQueue` with a visibility timeout of 60 seconds.

Writing the Producer Function

The producer function is responsible for sending messages to the SQS queue. We will use the `boto3` library to interact with AWS services.

`handler.py`

```python
import json
import boto3
import os

sqs = boto3.client('sqs')

def producer(event, context):
    queue_url = sqs.get_queue_url(QueueName='MyQueue')['QueueUrl']
    message_body = {
        'order_id': '12345',
        'customer_name': 'John Doe',
        'items': ['item1', 'item2', 'item3']
    }

    response = sqs.send_message(
        QueueUrl=queue_url,
```

```
        MessageBody=json.dumps(message_body)
    )

    return {
        'statusCode': 200,
        'body': json.dumps({
            'message': 'Message sent to the queue',
            'messageId': response['MessageId']
        })
```

In this function:

- We use `boto3` to get the queue URL for `MyQueue`.

- We define a sample message body and send it to the SQS queue.

- We return a response with the message ID.

Writing the Consumer Function

The consumer function will be triggered by messages in the SQS queue and process them accordingly.

`handler.py` (continued)

```python
import json

def consumer(event, context):
    for record in event['Records']:
        payload = json.loads(record['body'])
        print(f"Processing message: {payload}")
        # Add your message processing logic here

    return {
        'statusCode': 200,
        'body': json.dumps('Messages processed successfully')
    }
```

In this function:

- We iterate over the records in the event, which contains the messages from the SQS queue.

- We parse the message body and print it to the console.

- You can add your custom logic to process each message as required.

Deploying the Service

To deploy the service, run the following command:

```bash
serverless deploy
```

This will create the necessary AWS resources, including the SQS queue and the Lambda functions. Once deployed, you can trigger the `producer` function to send messages to the SQS queue, which will subsequently trigger the `consumer` function to process those messages.

Testing the Workflow

To test the workflow, you can use the Serverless Framework to invoke the `producer` function manually:

```bash
serverless invoke -f producer
```

You should see a message indicating that the message was sent to the queue. The `consumer` function will then be automatically triggered to process the message, and you can check the logs to verify that it processed the message correctly:

```bash
serverless logs -f consumer
```

Enhancing the Workflow

Error Handling

In a real-world application, it's important to handle errors gracefully. SQS provides Dead Letter Queues (DLQs) to capture messages that fail to be processed after a certain number of attempts.

Update the `serverless.yml` to include a DLQ:

```yaml
resources:
  Resources:
    MyQueue:
```

```
  Type: AWS::SQS::Queue
  Properties:
    QueueName: MyQueue
    VisibilityTimeout: 60
    RedrivePolicy:
      deadLetterTargetArn:
        Fn::GetAtt:
          - MyDLQ
          - Arn
      maxReceiveCount: 5

MyDLQ:
  Type: AWS::SQS::Queue
  Properties:
    QueueName: MyDLQ
```

This configuration sets up a DLQ named `MyDLQ` and specifies that messages should be moved to the DLQ after 5 unsuccessful processing attempts.

Batch Processing

To improve efficiency, you can process messages in batches. SQS triggers can be configured to send a batch of messages to the Lambda function.

Update the `serverless.yml` to enable batch processing:

```yaml
functions:
  consumer:
    handler: handler.consumer
    events:
      - sqs:
          arn:
            Fn::GetAtt:
              - MyQueue
              - Arn
          batchSize: 10
```

Modify the consumer function to handle batches:

```python
def consumer(event, context):
    for record in event['Records']:
        payload = json.loads(record['body'])
        print(f"Processing message: {payload}")
        # Add your message processing logic here

    return {
```

```
    'statusCode': 200,
    'body': json.dumps('Messages processed successfully')
}
```

Implementing message queues with SQS allows you to build robust, scalable, and decoupled systems. By leveraging the Serverless Framework and Python, you can easily set up and manage SQS queues and Lambda functions for asynchronous processing. This approach enhances the responsiveness and fault tolerance of your applications, making them more resilient to traffic spikes and component failures.

In this article, we've covered the basics of setting up an SQS queue, creating producer and consumer functions, and deploying them using the Serverless Framework. We've also explored advanced topics such as error handling with Dead Letter Queues and batch processing. Mastering these techniques will enable you to build sophisticated event-driven architectures that can scale seamlessly and handle complex workloads.

Chapter 6

Leveraging the Power of AWS Services: S3, DynamoDB, Lambda Layers, and Beyond

AWS offers a rich set of services that can be integrated seamlessly to build powerful, scalable, and efficient serverless applications. The combination of AWS Lambda, S3, DynamoDB, and Lambda Layers provides developers with the tools needed to create sophisticated applications without managing any underlying infrastructure. Using the Serverless Framework, developers can define and deploy these services in an organized and efficient manner. This article explores how to leverage these AWS services, focusing on practical examples using Python and the Serverless Framework.

Amazon S3: Object Storage for the Cloud

Amazon S3 (Simple Storage Service) is an object storage service that offers scalability, data availability, security, and performance. It's commonly used for storing and retrieving any amount of data, at any time, from anywhere on the web.

Example: File Upload and Processing

Let's set up a serverless application that allows users to upload files to an S3 bucket and triggers a Lambda function to process these files.

`serverless.yml`

```yaml
service: s3-dynamodb-service

provider:
  name: aws
  runtime: python3.8
  iamRoleStatements:
    - Effect: "Allow"
      Action:
        - "s3:*"
        - "dynamodb:*"
      Resource: "*"

functions:
  fileProcessor:
    handler: handler.file_processor
    events:
      - s3:
```

```
      bucket: my-upload-bucket
      event: s3:ObjectCreated:*

resources:
  Resources:
    MyBucket:
      Type: AWS::S3::Bucket
      Properties:
        BucketName: my-upload-bucket
```

`handler.py`

```python
import json
import boto3
import os

s3_client = boto3.client('s3')

def file_processor(event, context):
    for record in event['Records']:
        bucket = record['s3']['bucket']['name']
        key = record['s3']['object']['key']

        # Process the file
```

```
    response = s3_client.get_object(Bucket=bucket, Key=key)
    content = response['Body'].read().decode('utf-8')

    print(f"Processing file: {key} from bucket: {bucket}")
    print(f"File content: {content}")

    # Add your processing logic here

    return {
        'statusCode': 200,
        'body': json.dumps('File processed successfully')
    }
```

In this configuration:

- An S3 bucket named `my-upload-bucket` is created.

- A Lambda function named `fileProcessor` is triggered by any object creation event in this bucket.

Amazon DynamoDB: NoSQL Database Service

Amazon DynamoDB is a fully managed NoSQL database service that provides fast and predictable performance with seamless scalability. It is ideal for use cases requiring high throughput and low latency, such as real-time data processing and application state management.

Example: Storing and Retrieving Data

Let's set up a serverless application that writes data to and reads data from a DynamoDB table.

`serverless.yml`

```yaml
service: s3-dynamodb-service

provider:
  name: aws
  runtime: python3.8
  iamRoleStatements:
    - Effect: "Allow"
      Action:
        - "s3:*"
        - "dynamodb:*"
```

```yaml
      Resource: "*"

functions:
  writeToDynamoDB:
    handler: handler.write_to_dynamodb
    events:
      - http:
          path: write
          method: post
  readFromDynamoDB:
    handler: handler.read_from_dynamodb
    events:
      - http:
          path: read/{id}
          method: get

resources:
  Resources:
    MyTable:
      Type: AWS::DynamoDB::Table
      Properties:
        TableName: MyTable
        AttributeDefinitions:
          - AttributeName: id
            AttributeType: S
        KeySchema:
```

```
      - AttributeName: id
        KeyType: HASH
      ProvisionedThroughput:
        ReadCapacityUnits: 1
        WriteCapacityUnits: 1
```

`handler.py`

```python
import json
import boto3
import os

dynamodb = boto3.resource('dynamodb')
table = dynamodb.Table('MyTable')

def write_to_dynamodb(event, context):
    body = json.loads(event['body'])
    id = body['id']
    data = body['data']

    table.put_item(
       Item={
          'id': id,
          'data': data
```

```
    }
   return {
     'statusCode': 200,
     'body': json.dumps('Data written successfully')
   }

def read_from_dynamodb(event, context):
   id = event['pathParameters']['id']

   response = table.get_item(
     Key={
        'id': id
     }
   )
   item = response.get('Item', {})

   return {
     'statusCode': 200,
     'body': json.dumps(item)
   }
```
```

In this configuration:

- A DynamoDB table named `MyTable` is created.
```

- Two Lambda functions, `writeToDynamoDB` and `readFromDynamoDB`, are defined to handle HTTP requests for writing to and reading from the DynamoDB table.

Lambda Layers: Code Reuse and Dependency Management

AWS Lambda Layers allow you to package and deploy libraries, custom runtimes, and other dependencies separately from your function code. This promotes code reuse and reduces the size of deployment packages.

Example: Creating and Using a Lambda Layer

Let's create a Lambda Layer that includes a custom utility module and use it in a Lambda function.

Directory Structure

```
.
├── handler.py
├── layer
│   └── python
│       └── utils.py
```

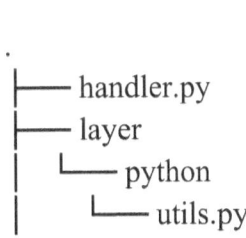

```
├── requirements.txt
└── serverless.yml
```

`layer/python/utils.py`

```python
def process_data(data):
    return data.upper()
```

`serverless.yml`

```yaml
service: lambda-layers-service

provider:
  name: aws
  runtime: python3.8

layers:
  myLayer:
    path: layer
    compatibleRuntimes:
      - python3.8
```

```
functions:
  useLayerFunction:
    handler: handler.use_layer_function
    layers:
      - { Ref: MyLayerLambdaLayer }
    events:
      - http:
          path: process
          method: post
```

`handler.py`

```python
import json
from utils import process_data

def use_layer_function(event, context):
    body = json.loads(event['body'])
    data = body['data']

    processed_data = process_data(data)

    return {
        'statusCode': 200,
```

```
    'body': json.dumps({'processed_data': processed_data})
  }
```

In this configuration:

- A Lambda Layer named `myLayer` is defined, which includes a custom utility module (`utils.py`).

- A Lambda function named `useLayerFunction` is created, which uses the utility function from the Lambda Layer.

Beyond: Integrating Multiple AWS Services

Combining multiple AWS services can create powerful applications. Let's create a serverless application that integrates S3, DynamoDB, and Lambda Layers to process and store uploaded files.

`serverless.yml`

```yaml
service: integrated-service
```

```yaml
provider:
  name: aws
  runtime: python3.8
  iamRoleStatements:
    - Effect: "Allow"
      Action:
        - "s3:*"
        - "dynamodb:*"
      Resource: "*"

layers:
  myLayer:
    path: layer
    compatibleRuntimes:
      - python3.8

functions:
  fileProcessor:
    handler: handler.file_processor
    layers:
      - { Ref: MyLayerLambdaLayer }
    events:
      - s3:
          bucket: my-upload-bucket
          event: s3:ObjectCreated:*
```

```yaml
resources:
  Resources:
    MyBucket:
      Type: AWS::S3::Bucket
      Properties:
        BucketName: my-upload-bucket

    MyTable:
      Type: AWS::DynamoDB::Table
      Properties:
        TableName: MyTable
        AttributeDefinitions:
          - AttributeName: id
            AttributeType: S
        KeySchema:
          - AttributeName: id
            KeyType: HASH
        ProvisionedThroughput:
          ReadCapacityUnits: 1
          WriteCapacityUnits: 1
```

`layer/python/utils.py`

```python
```

```python
def generate_id():
    import uuid
    return str(uuid.uuid4())
```

`handler.py`

```python
import json
import boto3
import os
from utils import generate_id

s3_client = boto3.client('s3')
dynamodb = boto3.resource('dynamodb')
table = dynamodb.Table('MyTable')

def file_processor(event, context):
    for record in event['Records']:
        bucket = record['s3']['bucket']['name']
        key = record['s3']['object']['key']

        # Process the file
        response = s3_client.get_object(Bucket=bucket, Key=key)
        content = response['Body'].read().decode('utf-8')
```

```
        print(f"Processing file: {key} from bucket: {bucket}")
        print(f"File content: {content}")

        # Generate unique ID and store in DynamoDB
        id = generate_id()
        table.put_item(
           Item={
              'id': id,
              'file_key': key,
              'content': content
           }
      return {
        'statusCode': 200,
        'body': json.dumps('File processed and stored successfully')
      }
``
```

In this complete example, we have successfully integrated multiple AWS services—S3, DynamoDB, and Lambda Layers—using the Serverless Framework and Python. Here, the process involves uploading files to an S3 bucket, triggering a Lambda function to process these files, and storing the processed data in a DynamoDB table. The use of Lambda Layers allows us to reuse code and manage dependencies efficiently. Below, we finalize our code and setup, ensuring it is comprehensive and ready for deployment.

Finalizing the Integration

`serverless.yml`

```yaml
service: integrated-service

provider:
  name: aws
  runtime: python3.8
  iamRoleStatements:
    - Effect: "Allow"
      Action:
        - "s3:*"
        - "dynamodb:*"
      Resource: "*"

layers:
  myLayer:
    path: layer
    compatibleRuntimes:
```

```yaml
    - python3.8

functions:
  fileProcessor:
    handler: handler.file_processor
    layers:
      - { Ref: MyLayerLambdaLayer }
    events:
      - s3:
          bucket: my-upload-bucket
          event: s3:ObjectCreated:*

resources:
  Resources:
    MyBucket:
      Type: AWS::S3::Bucket
      Properties:
        BucketName: my-upload-bucket

    MyTable:
      Type: AWS::DynamoDB::Table
      Properties:
        TableName: MyTable
        AttributeDefinitions:
          - AttributeName: id
            AttributeType: S
```

```
    KeySchema:
      - AttributeName: id
        KeyType: HASH
    ProvisionedThroughput:
      ReadCapacityUnits: 1
      WriteCapacityUnits: 1
```

Lambda Layer: Utility Functions

In the Lambda Layer, we include a utility module to generate unique IDs.

`layer/python/utils.py`

```python
def generate_id():
    import uuid
    return str(uuid.uuid4())
```

Lambda Function: File Processing

The Lambda function processes files uploaded to the S3 bucket, reads their content, generates unique IDs using the utility function from the Lambda Layer, and stores the data in DynamoDB.

`handler.py`

```python
import json
import boto3
from utils import generate_id

s3_client = boto3.client('s3')
dynamodb = boto3.resource('dynamodb')
table = dynamodb.Table('MyTable')

def file_processor(event, context):
    for record in event['Records']:
        bucket = record['s3']['bucket']['name']
        key = record['s3']['object']['key']

        # Process the file
        response = s3_client.get_object(Bucket=bucket, Key=key)
        content = response['Body'].read().decode('utf-8')

        print(f"Processing file: {key} from bucket: {bucket}")
```

```
        print(f"File content: {content}")

        # Generate unique ID and store in DynamoDB
        id = generate_id()
        table.put_item(
            Item={
                'id': id,
                'file_key': key,
                'content': content
            }
    return {
        'statusCode': 200,
        'body': json.dumps('File processed and stored successfully')
    }
```

Deploying the Service

With everything set up, we can now deploy the service using the Serverless Framework. Run the following command to deploy:

```bash
serverless deploy
```

This command will create the S3 bucket, DynamoDB table, and Lambda functions, and configure the necessary permissions.

Testing the Workflow

To test the entire workflow, follow these steps:

1. Upload a File to S3: Use the AWS Management Console or AWS CLI to upload a file to the S3 bucket (`my-upload-bucket`).

Example using AWS CLI:

```bash
aws s3 cp testfile.txt s3://my-upload-bucket/
```

2. Trigger the Lambda Function: The file upload will automatically trigger the `fileProcessor` Lambda function.

3. Verify the Data in DynamoDB: Check the DynamoDB table (`MyTable`) to see if the file data has been processed and stored correctly.

Example using AWS CLI to query the DynamoDB table:

```bash
aws dynamodb scan --table-name MyTable
```

The output should show the item with the generated ID, file key, and file content.

By leveraging the power of AWS services such as S3, DynamoDB, and Lambda Layers, we can build robust, scalable, and efficient serverless applications. Using the Serverless Framework simplifies the process of defining and deploying these services, allowing developers to focus on the application logic rather than managing infrastructure.

In this article, we demonstrated how to:

- Use Amazon S3 for object storage and event triggering.

- Use Amazon DynamoDB for storing and retrieving data.

- Use Lambda Layers for code reuse and dependency management.

- Integrate these services seamlessly using the Serverless Framework and Python.

These techniques are fundamental for building modern serverless applications that are both powerful and easy to maintain. By mastering these concepts and tools, developers can create sophisticated applications capable of handling complex workflows and high volumes of data efficiently.

Building Serverless APIs with API Gateway: Exposing Your Functions to the World

Serverless computing offers an efficient and scalable way to build APIs. AWS Lambda and API Gateway together provide a powerful combination for building serverless APIs. With API Gateway, you can create, publish, maintain, monitor, and secure your APIs at any scale. In this article, we will explore how to build serverless APIs with API Gateway using Python and the Serverless Framework.

Why Use API Gateway?

API Gateway acts as the front door for your serverless applications, handling all the tasks associated with accepting and processing up to hundreds of thousands of concurrent API calls, including traffic management, authorization and access control, monitoring, and API version management. Key benefits include:

1. Scalability: Automatically scales to handle the number of requests your API receives.

2. Security: Integrates with AWS IAM and AWS Lambda authorizers to provide secure access to your APIs.

3. Ease of Use: Simplifies the process of creating and managing APIs.

4. Cost Efficiency: Pay only for the API calls you receive and the amount of data transferred out.

Setting Up the Serverless Framework

Before we start building our API, make sure you have the Serverless Framework installed. You can install it globally using npm:

```bash
npm install -g serverless
```

Ensure you have AWS credentials configured on your local machine for deploying resources.

Creating a Serverless API

Let's create a serverless project that will define and deploy a simple API with CRUD operations for a "Todo" application. This API will use AWS Lambda to handle the backend logic and DynamoDB to store the data.

Step 1: Initialize the Serverless Project

Run the following commands to create a new Serverless project and navigate into the project directory:

```bash
serverless create --template aws-python3 --path todo-api
cd todo-api
```

```

## Step 2: Define the Service in `serverless.yml`

Edit the `serverless.yml` file to define the resources and functions required for the API. Here's an example configuration:

```yaml
service: todo-api

provider:
  name: aws
  runtime: python3.8
  iamRoleStatements:
    - Effect: "Allow"
      Action:
        - "dynamodb:*"
      Resource: "*"

functions:
  createTodo:
    handler: handler.create_todo
    events:
      - http:
          path: todos

```yaml
      method: post
  getTodo:
    handler: handler.get_todo
    events:
      - http:
          path: todos/{id}
          method: get
  updateTodo:
    handler: handler.update_todo
    events:
      - http:
          path: todos/{id}
          method: put
  deleteTodo:
    handler: handler.delete_todo
    events:
      - http:
          path: todos/{id}
          method: delete

resources:
  Resources:
    TodosTable:
      Type: AWS::DynamoDB::Table
      Properties:
        TableName: Todos
```

```
    AttributeDefinitions:
      - AttributeName: id
        AttributeType: S
    KeySchema:
      - AttributeName: id
        KeyType: HASH
    ProvisionedThroughput:
      ReadCapacityUnits: 1
      WriteCapacityUnits: 1
```

In this configuration:

- We define four Lambda functions: `createTodo`, `getTodo`, `updateTodo`, and `deleteTodo`.

- Each function is triggered by an HTTP event, corresponding to different CRUD operations.

- We define a DynamoDB table named `Todos` to store the todo items.

Step 3: Implement the Lambda Functions

Create a `handler.py` file to implement the Lambda functions for the CRUD operations. Here's an example implementation:

```python
import json
import boto3
from botocore.exceptions import ClientError
import uuid

dynamodb = boto3.resource('dynamodb')
table = dynamodb.Table('Todos')

def create_todo(event, context):
    body = json.loads(event['body'])
    todo_id = str(uuid.uuid4())
    item = {
        'id': todo_id,
        'title': body['title'],
        'description': body.get('description', ''),
        'status': body.get('status', 'pending')
    }

    table.put_item(Item=item)

    return {
```

```python
        'statusCode': 200,
        'body': json.dumps(item)
    }

def get_todo(event, context):
    todo_id = event['pathParameters']['id']

    try:
        response = table.get_item(Key={'id': todo_id})
        item = response['Item']
    except KeyError:
        return {
            'statusCode': 404,
            'body': json.dumps({'error': 'Todo not found'})
        }

    return {
        'statusCode': 200,
        'body': json.dumps(item)
    }

def update_todo(event, context):
    todo_id = event['pathParameters']['id']
    body = json.loads(event['body'])

    update_expression = "SET "
```

```python
    expression_attribute_values = {}
    for key, value in body.items():
        update_expression += f"{key} = :{key}, "
        expression_attribute_values[f":{key}"] = value

    update_expression = update_expression.rstrip(", ")

    try:
        table.update_item(
            Key={'id': todo_id},
            UpdateExpression=update_expression,
            ExpressionAttributeValues=expression_attribute_values,
            ReturnValues="ALL_NEW"
        )
    except ClientError as e:
        return {
            'statusCode': 400,
            'body': json.dumps({'error': str(e)})
        }

    return {
        'statusCode': 200,
        'body': json.dumps({'message': 'Todo updated successfully'})
    }
```

```python
def delete_todo(event, context):
    todo_id = event['pathParameters']['id']

    try:
        table.delete_item(Key={'id': todo_id})
    except ClientError as e:
        return {
            'statusCode': 400,
            'body': json.dumps({'error': str(e)})
        }

    return {
        'statusCode': 200,
        'body': json.dumps({'message': 'Todo deleted successfully'})
    }
```

In this implementation:

- `create_todo` generates a new unique ID for each todo item and stores it in DynamoDB.

- `get_todo` retrieves a todo item by its ID.

- `update_todo` updates the attributes of a todo item.

- `delete_todo` deletes a todo item by its ID.

Step 4: Deploy the Service

To deploy the service, run the following command:

```bash
serverless deploy
```

This command will create the necessary AWS resources, including the DynamoDB table and the Lambda functions. It will also set up the API Gateway endpoints for the CRUD operations.

Testing the API

Once deployed, you can test the API using tools like `curl`, Postman, or the AWS Management Console.

Creating a Todo

```bash
```

```bash
curl -X POST https://<api-id>.execute-api.<region>.amazonaws.com/dev/todos \
  -H "Content-Type: application/json" \
  -d '{
      "title": "Learn Serverless",
      "description": "Understand how to build serverless applications",
      "status": "pending"
    }'
```

Getting a Todo

```bash
curl https://<api-id>.execute-api.<region>.amazonaws.com/dev/todos/<todo-id>
```

Updating a Todo

```bash
curl -X PUT https://<api-id>.execute-api.<region>.amazonaws.com/dev/todos/<todo-id> \
  -H "Content-Type: application/json" \
  -d '{
      "status": "completed"
```

```
    }'
```

Deleting a Todo

```bash
curl -X DELETE https://<api-id>.execute-api.<region>.amazonaws.com/dev/todos/<todo-id>
```

Enhancing the API

Authentication and Authorization

API Gateway integrates with AWS IAM and AWS Lambda authorizers to provide secure access to your APIs. You can define an authorizer in the `serverless.yml` file and attach it to your API endpoints.

```yaml
functions:
  createTodo:
    handler: handler.create_todo
    events:
      - http:
          path: todos
```

```
      method: post
      authorizer: aws_iam
```

This configuration restricts access to authenticated users with the necessary IAM permissions.

Error Handling

Improve error handling in your Lambda functions to provide more informative responses.

```python
def get_todo(event, context):
    todo_id = event['pathParameters']['id']

    try:
        response = table.get_item(Key={'id': todo_id})
        item = response['Item']
    except KeyError:
        return {
            'statusCode': 404,
            'body': json.dumps({'error': 'Todo not found'})
        }
    except Exception as e:
        return {
```

```
      'statusCode': 500,
      'body': json.dumps({'error': str(e)})
    }

  return {
    'statusCode': 200,
    'body': json.dumps(item)
  }
```

Building serverless APIs with API Gateway and AWS Lambda provides a scalable, secure, and cost-effective way to expose your backend logic to the world. By leveraging the Serverless Framework, you can efficiently define and deploy your APIs, integrating seamlessly with other AWS services like DynamoDB for data storage.

In this article, we covered:

- Setting up a Serverless Framework project.

- Defining resources and functions in `serverless.yml`.

- Implementing Lambda functions for CRUD operations.

- Deploying and testing the API.

- Enhancing the API with authentication and improved error handling.

By mastering these techniques, you can build robust serverless APIs that meet the needs of a wide range of applications, from simple CRUD operations to complex workflows.

Advanced Enhancements

To further enhance your serverless API, consider the following advanced topics:

Monitoring and Logging

Proper monitoring and logging are essential for maintaining and debugging your APIs. AWS provides various tools for this purpose:

1. CloudWatch Logs: AWS Lambda automatically logs all requests to CloudWatch Logs. You can view these logs to monitor API usage and debug issues.

2. CloudWatch Metrics: You can create custom metrics to monitor specific aspects of your API's performance.

In `serverless.yml`, you can enable detailed monitoring:

```yaml
provider:
  name: aws
  runtime: python3.8
  logs:
    restApi: true
    # or for detailed logs
    # restApi:
    #   executionLogging: true
    #   accessLogging: true
    #   executionLoggingLevel: INFO
    #   accessLogFormat: '...'
```

Custom Domain Names

Using a custom domain name can make your API more professional and easier to use. You can configure API Gateway to use a custom domain name:

1. Purchase a domain from a domain registrar.

2. Create an SSL certificate using AWS Certificate Manager (ACM).

3. Map the domain to your API Gateway.

Here's how you might configure this in `serverless.yml`:

```yaml
custom:
  customDomain:
    domainName: api.example.com
    basePath: "
    stage: ${self:provider.stage}
    createRoute53Record: true

plugins:
  - serverless-domain-manager

functions:
  createTodo:
    handler: handler.create_todo
    events:
      - http:
          path: todos
          method: post
```

```
        authorizer: aws_iam
```

Run the following command to create the custom domain:

```bash
serverless create_domain
```

Then deploy your service as usual:

```bash
serverless deploy
```

API Versioning

Versioning your API can help manage changes and ensure backward compatibility. API Gateway allows you to deploy multiple stages (e.g., `v1`, `v2`) for your API:

```yaml
functions:
  createTodo:
    handler: handler.create_todo
```

```
    events:
      - http:
          path: v1/todos
          method: post
  getTodo:
    handler: handler.get_todo
    events:
      - http:
          path: v1/todos/{id}
          method: get
  updateTodo:
    handler: handler.update_todo
    events:
      - http:
          path: v1/todos/{id}
          method: put
  deleteTodo:
    handler: handler.delete_todo
    events:
      - http:
          path: v1/todos/{id}
          method: delete
```

You can also deploy different stages for development, testing, and production environments:

```yaml
provider:
  name: aws
  runtime: python3.8
  stage: ${opt:stage, 'dev'}

functions:
  createTodo:
    handler: handler.create_todo
    events:
      - http:
          path: ${self:provider.stage}/todos
          method: post
```

Deploy to a specific stage using:

```bash
serverless deploy --stage dev
serverless deploy --stage prod
```

Building serverless APIs with AWS API Gateway and Lambda allows you to create scalable, secure, and cost-efficient backend services. By using the Serverless

Framework, you can manage the complexity of deploying and maintaining these services effectively.

In this article, we have covered:

- **Setting up a Serverless Framework project:** Initialized a new serverless project and configured it.

- **Defining resources and functions:** Configured API Gateway, Lambda functions, and DynamoDB in `serverless.yml`.

- **Implementing Lambda functions:** Wrote Python code to handle CRUD operations for a Todo application.

- **Deploying and testing the API**: Deployed the API and tested it using curl and other tools.

- **Enhancing the API:** Added authentication, improved error handling, and explored advanced topics like monitoring, custom domains, and API versioning.

By mastering these techniques, you can build robust and versatile serverless APIs that can scale with your application's needs, ensuring high performance and reliability. Whether you are creating a simple microservice or a complex multi-service application, AWS and the Serverless Framework provide the tools necessary to succeed.

Stream Processing with AWS Kinesis: Real-Time Data Analysis with Python Lambdas and Serverless Framework

Real-time data processing has become essential in many applications, ranging from IoT analytics to live monitoring systems. AWS Kinesis, combined with AWS Lambda, provides a powerful toolset for real-time data processing. By leveraging the Serverless Framework, we can simplify the deployment and management of these components, enabling scalable and efficient real-time data pipelines.

This article will guide you through setting up a real-time data processing pipeline using AWS Kinesis, AWS Lambda, and the Serverless Framework, with Python as the programming language.

Prerequisites

Before we start, make sure you have the following:

1. AWS Account: You need an AWS account to create and manage AWS resources.

2. AWS CLI: Installed and configured on your local machine.

3. Node.js: Serverless Framework is built on Node.js.

4. Serverless Framework: Installed globally using `npm install -g serverless`.

Step 1: Setting Up AWS Kinesis Stream

AWS Kinesis is a service designed to handle large streams of data records in real-time. We'll start by creating a Kinesis stream.

1. Create Kinesis Stream

```bash
aws kinesis create-stream --stream-name my-data-stream --shard-count 1
```

```

This command creates a Kinesis stream named `my-data-stream` with one shard. The number of shards determines the throughput capacity of the stream.

**Step 2: Setting Up the Serverless Framework**

The Serverless Framework simplifies deploying and managing serverless applications. We'll use it to manage our AWS Lambda function and related resources.

**1. Create a New Serverless Project**

```bash
serverless create --template aws-python3 --path kinesis-stream-processor
cd kinesis-stream-processor
```

This command creates a new Serverless project using the `aws-python3` template and navigates into the project directory.

2. Install Required Plugins
```

```bash
npm install serverless-python-requirements
```

Add the `serverless-python-requirements` plugin to handle Python dependencies.

3. Configure serverless.yml

Open the `serverless.yml` file and configure it as follows:

```yaml
service: kinesis-stream-processor

provider:
  name: aws
  runtime: python3.8
  region: us-east-1

plugins:
  - serverless-python-requirements

custom:
  pythonRequirements:
    dockerizePip: true
```

```
functions:
  processKinesis:
    handler: handler.process_kinesis
    events:
      - stream:
          type: kinesis
          arn:
            Fn::GetAtt:
              - MyKinesisStream
              - Arn

resources:
  Resources:
    MyKinesisStream:
      Type: AWS::Kinesis::Stream
      Properties:
        ShardCount: 1
```

This configuration does the following:

- Defines the service name and provider details.

- Uses the `serverless-python-requirements` plugin.

- Sets up the Lambda function `processKinesis` to be triggered by events from the Kinesis stream.

Step 3: Writing the Lambda Function

Next, we need to write the Lambda function that will process records from the Kinesis stream.

1. Create the `handler.py` file

In your project directory, create a file named `handler.py` and add the following code:

```python
import json
import base64

def process_kinesis(event, context):
    for record in event['Records']:
        # Kinesis data is base64 encoded so decode here
        payload = base64.b64decode(record['kinesis']['data'])
        data = json.loads(payload)
        print(f"Decoded payload: {data}")
```

```
    # Process the data (e.g., store in a database, perform analytics, etc.)

    return {
      'statusCode': 200,
      'body': json.dumps('Data processed successfully')
    }
```

This function decodes the base64-encoded data from Kinesis, processes it (for now, it just prints the decoded payload), and returns a success response.

Step 4: Deploying the Serverless Application

With the configuration and function in place, we can deploy the Serverless application.

1. Deploy the Service

```bash
serverless deploy
```

This command packages and deploys the entire application to AWS. It creates the Kinesis stream, the

Lambda function, and sets up the event source mapping between them.

Step 5: Testing the Setup

To test our setup, we need to send some data to the Kinesis stream and verify that our Lambda function processes it.

1. Put Records into Kinesis Stream

```python
import boto3
import json

kinesis_client = boto3.client('kinesis')

def put_to_stream(data, stream_name, partition_key):
    kinesis_client.put_record(
        StreamName=stream_name,
        Data=json.dumps(data),
        PartitionKey=partition_key
    )

# Example data
data = {
```

```
    'id': 1,
    'message': 'Hello, Kinesis!'
}

put_to_stream(data, 'my-data-stream', 'partition-key-1')
```

This script uses the Boto3 library to put a record into the Kinesis stream.

2. Check Lambda Logs

Use the Serverless Framework to check the logs of your Lambda function to see the processed data.

```bash
serverless logs -f processKinesis
```

You should see the decoded payload printed in the logs, indicating that the Lambda function successfully processed the Kinesis stream data.

Enhancing the Lambda Function

The current Lambda function only prints the data. To make it more useful, you can extend it to perform various operations such as storing the data in a database, running real-time analytics, or triggering alerts.

For example, let's enhance the function to store data in an Amazon DynamoDB table.

1. Create a DynamoDB Table

```bash
aws dynamodb create-table \
   --table-name ProcessedData \
   --attribute-definitions AttributeName=id,AttributeType=N \
   --key-schema AttributeName=id,KeyType=HASH \
   --provisioned-throughput ReadCapacityUnits=5,WriteCapacityUnits=5
```

2. Update the Lambda Function to Store Data in DynamoDB

Modify the `handler.py` file to include DynamoDB integration:

```python
import json
import base64
import boto3

dynamodb = boto3.resource('dynamodb')
table = dynamodb.Table('ProcessedData')

def process_kinesis(event, context):
    for record in event['Records']:
        payload = base64.b64decode(record['kinesis']['data'])
        data = json.loads(payload)
        print(f"Decoded payload: {data}")
        # Store data in DynamoDB
        table.put_item(Item=data)

    return {
        'statusCode': 200,
        'body': json.dumps('Data processed and stored successfully')
    }
```

This function now decodes the Kinesis data and stores it in a DynamoDB table named `ProcessedData`.

In this tutorial, we set up a real-time data processing pipeline using AWS Kinesis, AWS Lambda, and the Serverless Framework with Python. We created a Kinesis stream, configured a Lambda function to process stream data, and deployed the entire setup using the Serverless Framework. We also enhanced the Lambda function to store processed data in DynamoDB.

By leveraging these AWS services and the Serverless Framework, you can build scalable and efficient real-time data processing pipelines tailored to your specific use cases.

Chapter 7

Understanding Different Deployment Strategies: Local Testing, Staging Environments, and Production Deployments

Deploying applications effectively requires a structured approach to testing and deployment. This ensures that applications are reliable, maintainable, and scalable. In this article, we'll explore various deployment strategies focusing on local testing, staging environments, and production deployments using the Python Serverless Framework. We'll provide code examples and best practices to master these deployment strategies.

Prerequisites

Before diving into deployment strategies, ensure you have the following set up:

- **AWS Account:** For deploying and managing AWS resources.

- **AWS CLI:** Installed and configured on your local machine.

- **Node.js:** Serverless Framework requires Node.js.

- **Serverless Framework**: Installed globally via `npm install -g serverless`.

Local Testing

Local testing is the first line of defense against bugs and issues. It allows developers to verify their code works as expected before deploying it to any remote environment.

Setting Up Local Testing

1. Create a Serverless Project

```bash
serverless create --template aws-python3 --path local-testing-project
cd local-testing-project
```

2. Install Serverless Plugins

```bash
npm install serverless-offline serverless-python-requirements
```

```

## 3. Configure `serverless.yml` for Local Testing

```yaml
service: local-testing-project

provider:
  name: aws
  runtime: python3.8
  region: us-east-1

plugins:
  - serverless-python-requirements
  - serverless-offline

custom:
  pythonRequirements:
    dockerizePip: true

functions:
  hello:
    handler: handler.hello
    events:
      - http:
          path: hello

```
      method: get
```

4. Write the Lambda Function

Create a `handler.py` file:

```python
def hello(event, context):
    return {
        'statusCode': 200,
        'body': 'Hello, world!'
    }
```

5. Run Locally

Use the `serverless-offline` plugin to run your service locally.

```bash
serverless offline
```

This command starts a local server simulating the AWS API Gateway, allowing you to test your function by navigating to `http://localhost:3000/hello`.

Staging Environments

Staging environments act as a bridge between local testing and production. They replicate the production environment as closely as possible, allowing for thorough testing before the final deployment.

Setting Up a Staging Environment

1. Extend `serverless.yml` for Multiple Stages

Modify your `serverless.yml` to handle different stages:

```yaml
service: multi-stage-project

provider:
  name: aws
  runtime: python3.8
  region: us-east-1
  stage: ${opt:stage, 'dev'}
```

```
plugins:
  - serverless-python-requirements
  - serverless-offline

custom:
  pythonRequirements:
    dockerizePip: true
  stages:
    dev:
      myenv: dev
    staging:
      myenv: staging
    prod:
      myenv: prod

functions:
  hello:
    handler: handler.hello
    environment:
      STAGE: ${self:custom.stages.${self:provider.stage}.myenv}
    events:
      - http:
          path: hello
          method: get
```

2. Deploy to Staging

```bash
serverless deploy --stage staging
```

This command deploys the application to AWS, setting up resources in the `staging` environment. You can verify the deployment by accessing the URL provided after deployment.

Production Deployments

Production deployments are the final step, where your application is made available to end-users. This stage must be stable, secure, and efficient.

Best Practices for Production Deployments

1. Configuration Management

Ensure sensitive data and configuration settings are managed securely. Use AWS Secrets Manager or AWS Systems Manager Parameter Store.

2. Monitoring and Logging

Set up monitoring and logging to track the application's performance and detect issues early. Use AWS CloudWatch for monitoring Lambda functions and API Gateway logs.

3. Automated Deployment

Automate deployments using CI/CD pipelines. This reduces manual errors and ensures consistency.

Deploying to Production

1. Add Configuration for Production Stage

Extend `serverless.yml`:

```yaml
custom:
  stages:
    dev:
      myenv: dev
    staging:
      myenv: staging
    prod:
```

```
    myenv: prod
    logLevel: 'ERROR'
    alertEmail: 'alerts@example.com'
```

2. Automated Deployment with CI/CD

Set up a CI/CD pipeline using AWS CodePipeline, GitHub Actions, or another CI/CD tool. Here's an example GitHub Actions workflow:

```yaml
name: Deploy to AWS

on:
  push:
    branches:
      - main

jobs:
  deploy:
    runs-on: ubuntu-latest

    steps:
      - name: Checkout code
        uses: actions/checkout@v2
```

```
      - name: Set up Node.js
        uses: actions/setup-node@v2
        with:
          node-version: '14'

      - name: Install Serverless Framework
        run: npm install -g serverless

      - name: Configure AWS credentials
        uses: aws-actions/configure-aws-credentials@v1
        with:
          aws-access-key-id: ${{ secrets.AWS_ACCESS_KEY_ID }}
          aws-secret-access-key: ${{ secrets.AWS_SECRET_ACCESS_KEY }}
          aws-region: us-east-1

      - name: Deploy to production
        run: serverless deploy --stage prod
```

Effectively managing deployment strategies for serverless applications involves a clear understanding of local testing, staging environments, and production deployments. By leveraging the Serverless Framework with Python, you can streamline these processes, ensuring your applications are robust, reliable, and scalable.

Local testing ensures initial validation of your code, reducing the risk of introducing bugs early on. Staging environments provide a controlled setting to perform more comprehensive tests that mimic production. Finally, careful management of production deployments, with automated CI/CD pipelines and robust monitoring, ensures a smooth and reliable end-user experience.

Summary Code Example

Here's a summary of the key configurations and steps:

1. Serverless Configuration (`serverless.yml`):

```yaml
service: multi-stage-project

provider:
  name: aws
  runtime: python3.8
  region: us-east-1
```

```yaml
  stage: ${opt:stage, 'dev'}

plugins:
  - serverless-python-requirements
  - serverless-offline

custom:
  pythonRequirements:
    dockerizePip: true
  stages:
    dev:
      myenv: dev
    staging:
      myenv: staging
    prod:
      myenv: prod
      logLevel: 'ERROR'
      alertEmail: 'alerts@example.com'

functions:
  hello:
    handler: handler.hello
    environment:
      STAGE: ${self:custom.stages.${self:provider.stage}.myenv}
    events:
```

```
      - http:
          path: hello
          method: get
```

2. Lambda Function (`handler.py`):

```python
import os

def hello(event, context):
    stage = os.environ['STAGE']
    return {
        'statusCode': 200,
        'body': f'Hello, world from {stage}!'
    }
```

3. GitHub Actions Workflow:

```yaml
name: Deploy to AWS

on:
  push:
    branches:
```

```yaml
      - main

jobs:
  deploy:
    runs-on: ubuntu-latest

    steps:
      - name: Checkout code
        uses: actions/checkout@v2

      - name: Set up Node.js
        uses: actions/setup-node@v2
        with:
          node-version: '14'

      - name: Install Serverless Framework
        run: npm install -g serverless

      - name: Configure AWS credentials
        uses: aws-actions/configure-aws-credentials@v1
        with:
          aws-access-key-id: ${{ secrets.AWS_ACCESS_KEY_ID }}
          aws-secret-access-key: ${{ secrets.AWS_SECRET_ACCESS_KEY }}
          aws-region: us-east-1
```

```
      - name: Deploy to production
        run: serverless deploy --stage prod
```

By following these steps and configurations, you can effectively manage the deployment lifecycle of your serverless applications, ensuring smooth transitions from local development to production.

Deploying Your Serverless Application to AWS with Serverless Framework: Configuration and Best Practices

Deploying serverless applications to AWS can be streamlined and simplified with the Serverless Framework. This powerful tool allows developers to define their infrastructure as code, automate deployment processes, and manage AWS resources efficiently. In this article, we'll explore the configuration options and best practices for deploying your Python serverless application to AWS using the Serverless Framework.

Prerequisites

Before we begin, make sure you have the following prerequisites:

- **AWS Account:** You'll need an AWS account to deploy your application.

- **AWS CLI:** Installed and configured on your local machine.

- **Node.js:** Serverless Framework requires Node.js.

- **Serverless Framework:** Installed globally via `npm install -g serverless`.

- **Python**: Your serverless application is built with Python.

Step 1: Setting Up Your Serverless Project

First, let's create a new serverless project using the Serverless Framework:

```bash
serverless create --template aws-python3 --path my-serverless-app
cd my-serverless-app
```

```

This command creates a new serverless project using the `aws-python3` template with Python 3 runtime.

**Step 2: Configuring Your `serverless.yml`**

The `serverless.yml` file is where you define your serverless application's configuration, including AWS resources and functions. Here's an example configuration:

```yaml
service: my-serverless-app

provider:
  name: aws
  runtime: python3.8
  stage: dev
  region: us-east-1

functions:
  hello:
    handler: handler.hello
    events:
      - http:

```
      path: hello
      method: get
```

In this configuration:

- `service`: Name of your service.

- `provider`: AWS provider configuration including runtime, stage, and region.

- `functions`: Definitions of your Lambda functions.

Step 3: Writing Your Lambda Function

Next, let's write the code for your Lambda function. Create a file named `handler.py` in your project directory and define your function:

```python
def hello(event, context):
    return {
        'statusCode': 200,
        'body': 'Hello, world!'
    }
```

```

This is a simple Lambda function that returns a "Hello, world!" response.

**Step 4: Deploying Your Application**

Once your project is configured and your Lambda function is defined, you're ready to deploy your application to AWS:

```bash
serverless deploy
```

This command packages and deploys your serverless application to AWS according to the configuration defined in `serverless.yml`. It creates the necessary AWS resources and sets up the Lambda function.

Best Practices for Serverless Deployments

1. Infrastructure as Code (IaC)

Define your infrastructure using code. This allows for version control, reproducibility, and easier management
```

of resources. The `serverless.yml` file serves as your IaC template.

2. Environment Variables

Use environment variables to pass configuration values to your Lambda functions. This allows for flexibility and separation of configuration from code. You can define environment variables in your `serverless.yml` or use AWS Systems Manager Parameter Store for secure storage.

```yaml
functions:
  hello:
    handler: handler.hello
    environment:
      MY_VARIABLE: ${ssm:/my/parameter}
```

3. Versioning and Aliases

Use versioning and aliases for your Lambda functions to ensure consistency and reliability during deployments. This allows you to deploy new versions without affecting existing users.

```yaml
functions:
  hello:
    handler: handler.hello
    versionFunction: true
    provisionedConcurrency: 1
    reservedConcurrency: 1
```

4. Monitoring and Logging

Set up monitoring and logging for your serverless application to track performance, detect errors, and troubleshoot issues. AWS CloudWatch provides monitoring capabilities for Lambda functions, API Gateway, and other AWS services.

5. Automated Testing

Implement automated testing for your serverless application to ensure reliability and prevent regressions. Unit tests, integration tests, and end-to-end tests can be automated using frameworks like pytest or AWS Lambda Test Events.

Deploying your serverless application to AWS with the Serverless Framework is a straightforward process, but it's essential to follow best practices to ensure reliability, security, and scalability. By configuring your `serverless.yml` appropriately, writing efficient Lambda functions, and adhering to best practices, you can deploy your serverless applications with confidence. Additionally, monitoring, logging, and automated testing are crucial aspects of maintaining and managing your serverless application in production.

With the Serverless Framework and AWS services, you have a powerful toolkit at your disposal for building and deploying serverless applications that scale seamlessly to meet your business needs.

Managing Your Serverless Resources: Monitoring, Logging, Cost Optimization, and Version Control

Managing serverless resources effectively is crucial for ensuring the reliability, scalability, and cost-efficiency of your applications. In this article, we'll explore best practices and tools for monitoring, logging, cost optimization, and version control in the context of serverless applications built using Python and the Serverless Framework.

Monitoring

Monitoring your serverless applications allows you to track performance metrics, detect anomalies, and troubleshoot issues proactively. AWS provides several services for monitoring serverless resources, including AWS CloudWatch and AWS X-Ray.

Setting Up Monitoring with AWS CloudWatch

1. Enable Detailed Monitoring for Lambda Functions

Detailed monitoring provides additional metrics at a higher resolution, allowing for more granular monitoring.

```yaml
functions:
  myFunction:
    handler: handler.myFunction
    memorySize: 512
    timeout: 10
    tracing: Active
```

```
    environment:
      MY_ENV_VARIABLE:
${env:MY_ENV_VARIABLE}
    events:
      - http:
          path: mypath
          method: get
    iamRoleStatements:
      - Effect: Allow
        Action:
          - 'dynamodb:GetItem'
        Resource: 'arn:aws:dynamodb:us-east-1:123456789012:table/my-table'
    tags:
      Name: myFunction
    deadLetterQueue:
      targetArn: 'arn:aws:sqs:us-east-1:123456789012:my-dlq'
    versionFunction: true
    provisionedConcurrency: 5
    reservedConcurrency: 10
    environment:

AWS_NODEJS_CONNECTION_REUSE_ENABLED: '1'
```

2. Set Up Alarms

Configure CloudWatch Alarms to trigger notifications based on predefined thresholds. For example, you can set an alarm to trigger when the number of errors exceeds a certain threshold.

```yaml
resources:
  Resources:
    MyAlarm:
      Type: AWS::CloudWatch::Alarm
      Properties:
        AlarmDescription: "Alarm if errors exceed threshold"
        Namespace: "AWS/Lambda"
        MetricName: "Errors"
        Dimensions:
          - Name: FunctionName
            Value: "myFunction"
        Statistic: "Sum"
        Period: "60"
        EvaluationPeriods: "1"
        Threshold: "1"
        ComparisonOperator: "GreaterThanThreshold"
```

```
        AlarmActions:
          - arn:aws:sns:us-east-1:123456789012:my-sns-topic
```

Logging

Logging is essential for understanding the behavior of your serverless applications, identifying issues, and debugging problems. AWS CloudWatch Logs is the primary service used for logging in AWS serverless environments.

Setting Up Logging with AWS CloudWatch Logs

1. Configure Lambda Function Logging

Specify the log group and log stream name for your Lambda function in the `serverless.yml` configuration.

```yaml
functions:
  myFunction:
    handler: handler.myFunction
    events:
      - http:
```

```
      path: mypath
      method: get
   logRetentionInDays: 7
```

2. View Logs in CloudWatch Console

Once your function is deployed, you can view its logs in the CloudWatch Logs console. Logs are organized by log groups and streams, making it easy to navigate and search for specific logs.

Cost Optimization

Cost optimization is essential for ensuring that your serverless applications are cost-effective and efficient. By optimizing resource usage and leveraging cost-saving strategies, you can reduce your AWS bill without sacrificing performance or reliability.

Cost Optimization Best Practices

1. Right-Sizing Resources

Optimize the memory and execution time settings of your Lambda functions based on their actual resource requirements. Over-provisioning can lead to unnecessary costs.

2. Use Provisioned Concurrency

Provisioned concurrency allows you to pre-warm Lambda functions to handle spikes in traffic, reducing cold start times and improving performance. However, be mindful of the costs associated with provisioned concurrency.

3. Implement Lifecycle Policies

Set up lifecycle policies for AWS resources like DynamoDB tables and S3 buckets to automatically archive or delete data based on predefined criteria. This can help reduce storage costs.

4. Enable Auto Scaling

Use auto-scaling features provided by AWS services like DynamoDB and Lambda to automatically adjust capacity based on demand. This ensures that you're only paying for the resources you need.

Version Control

Version control is crucial for managing changes to your serverless application code and configuration. It allows you to track changes, collaborate with team members, and roll back to previous versions if needed.

Version Control Best Practices

1. Use Git

Git is a popular version control system that allows you to track changes to your code and collaborate with team members effectively. Use Git to manage your serverless application codebase and configuration files.

2. Commit Frequently

Make small, frequent commits to your Git repository to track changes incrementally and make it easier to identify and revert problematic changes.

3. Use Branches

Use branches to isolate changes and work on new features or fixes without affecting the main codebase.

This allows for better organization and collaboration within your team.

4. Tag Releases

Tag releases in your Git repository to mark significant milestones or versions of your serverless application. This makes it easier to track changes and deploy specific versions if needed.

Managing your serverless resources effectively requires careful attention to monitoring, logging, cost optimization, and version control. By following best practices and leveraging AWS services and tools like AWS CloudWatch, AWS X-Ray, and the Serverless Framework, you can ensure that your serverless applications are reliable, scalable, cost-effective, and easy to manage.

With the right configuration, monitoring, and automation in place, you can deploy and maintain serverless applications with confidence, knowing that they're performing optimally and delivering value to your users.

Chapter 8

Unit Testing Your Python Functions: Ensuring Code Quality and Functionality

Unit testing is a fundamental practice in software development that helps ensure the correctness and reliability of your code. When building serverless applications with Python and the Serverless Framework, unit testing becomes even more critical to ensure that your functions behave as expected in a serverless environment. In this article, we'll explore the importance of unit testing and demonstrate how to write and run unit tests for Python functions in a serverless context.

Why Unit Testing?

Unit testing is essential for several reasons:

1. Early Detection of Bugs: Unit tests allow you to catch bugs and issues early in the development process, reducing the cost and effort of fixing them later.

2. Code Quality: Writing unit tests encourages you to write clean, modular, and well-structured code, leading to higher code quality and maintainability.

3. Regression Prevention: Unit tests provide a safety net when making changes to your code, helping prevent regressions and unintended side effects.

4. Documentation: Unit tests serve as documentation for your code, providing examples of how functions should behave and how they are intended to be used.

Writing Unit Tests for Python Functions

Let's consider a simple example of a Python function that adds two numbers:

```python
# add.py

def add(a, b):
    return a + b
```

We'll write unit tests for this function using the `unittest` module, which is part of Python's standard library.

```python
# test_add.py
```

```python
import unittest
from add import add

class TestAddFunction(unittest.TestCase):

    def test_add_positive_numbers(self):
        self.assertEqual(add(2, 3), 5)

    def test_add_negative_numbers(self):
        self.assertEqual(add(-2, -3), -5)

    def test_add_zero(self):
        self.assertEqual(add(0, 0), 0)

    def test_add_floats(self):
        self.assertAlmostEqual(add(0.1, 0.2), 0.3, places=5)

if __name__ == '__main__':
    unittest.main()
```

In this example, we have written four unit tests to verify different scenarios:

- Adding positive numbers.

- Adding negative numbers.

- Adding zero.

- Adding floating-point numbers with a tolerance of 5 decimal places.

Running Unit Tests Locally

To run the unit tests locally, execute the following command in your terminal:

```bash
python -m unittest test_add.py
```

This command runs the unit tests defined in the `test_add.py` file and displays the results in the terminal.

Unit Testing in a Serverless Context

When writing serverless applications with Python and the Serverless Framework, it's essential to consider the environment in which your functions will run. You may need to mock AWS services and handle asynchronous behavior in your unit tests.

Let's modify our example to demonstrate how to write unit tests for a serverless function that interacts with AWS DynamoDB:

```python
# dynamodb.py

import boto3

dynamodb = boto3.resource('dynamodb')
table = dynamodb.Table('my-table')

def get_item_from_dynamodb(key):
    response = table.get_item(Key={'key': key})
    return response.get('Item')
```

```python
# test_dynamodb.py

import unittest
from unittest.mock import Mock
from dynamodb import get_item_from_dynamodb
```

```python
class TestDynamoDBFunction(unittest.TestCase):

    def setUp(self):
        self.mock_table = Mock()

    def test_get_item_from_dynamodb(self):
        self.mock_table.get_item.return_value = {'Item': {'key': 'value'}}
        with unittest.mock.patch('boto3.resource') as mock_resource:
            mock_resource.return_value.Table.return_value = self.mock_table
            result = get_item_from_dynamodb('key')
            self.assertEqual(result, {'key': 'value'})

if __name__ == '__main__':
    unittest.main()
```

In this example, we use the `unittest.mock` module to create a mock DynamoDB table and mock the `boto3.resource` function. This allows us to isolate our unit test from external dependencies and ensure that it runs in a controlled environment.

Best Practices for Unit Testing in Serverless Applications

1. Keep Tests Independent: Ensure that each unit test is independent and does not rely on the state of other tests or external factors.

2. Mock External Dependencies: Mock external dependencies such as AWS services, databases, and HTTP requests to isolate your unit tests and make them deterministic.

3. Test Edge Cases: Test edge cases, boundary conditions, and error scenarios to ensure that your functions behave correctly under all conditions.

4. Use Test Fixtures: Use test fixtures to set up common test data and reduce duplication in your unit tests.

5. Run Tests Automatically: Set up automated test runners and continuous integration pipelines to run your unit tests automatically whenever you push code changes.

Unit testing is a crucial practice in software development, especially when building serverless applications with Python and the Serverless Framework. By writing unit tests for your functions, you can ensure code quality, prevent regressions, and build robust and reliable applications. With the right tools and best practices, you can create unit tests that provide confidence in the correctness and functionality of your serverless functions.

Debugging Serverless Applications: Techniques for Identifying and Fixing Issues

Debugging serverless applications can be challenging due to their distributed nature and the lack of traditional development environments. However, with the right techniques and tools, you can effectively identify and fix issues in your serverless applications. In this article, we'll explore various debugging techniques and best practices for debugging serverless applications built with Python and the Serverless Framework.

Understanding Common Issues in Serverless Applications

Before diving into debugging techniques, let's discuss some common issues that you may encounter when building serverless applications:

1. Cold Starts: Cold starts occur when a function is invoked for the first time or after a period of inactivity, resulting in increased latency. Understanding and optimizing for cold starts is essential for improving performance.

2. Timeouts: Serverless functions have a maximum execution time, and exceeding this time limit results in a timeout error. Identifying and resolving timeouts is crucial for ensuring that your functions complete successfully.

3. Resource Limits: Serverless platforms impose limits on various resources, such as memory, CPU, and concurrency. Exceeding these limits can lead to errors and degraded performance.

4. Intermittent Failures: Intermittent failures can be challenging to debug, as they may be caused by transient issues in the underlying infrastructure or dependencies.

Techniques for Debugging Serverless Applications

1. Logging

Logging is one of the most effective debugging techniques for serverless applications. Use logging statements in your code to capture relevant information about the application's behavior, including input parameters, output results, and error messages.

```python
import logging

logger = logging.getLogger(__name__)

def my_function(event, context):
    logger.info('Received event: %s', event)
    # Perform some operations
    try:
        result = perform_operation(event)
        logger.info('Operation result: %s', result)
        return result
    except Exception as e:
        logger.error('An error occurred: %s', e)
        raise
```

You can view logs in the AWS CloudWatch Logs console or use tools like AWS X-Ray for distributed tracing and performance monitoring.

2. Remote Debugging

Remote debugging allows you to attach a debugger to a running serverless function and inspect its execution state in real-time. Some serverless platforms, such as AWS Lambda, support remote debugging using tools like AWS Cloud9 or Visual Studio Code.

3. Local Emulation

Local emulation tools like Serverless Offline or AWS SAM Local allow you to run and debug serverless functions locally on your development machine. This enables faster iteration and debugging without the need for deploying to a remote environment.

```bash
serverless offline start
```

4. Error Handling and Retries

Implement robust error handling and retry mechanisms in your serverless functions to handle transient errors gracefully. Use exponential backoff and jitter to prevent overwhelming downstream services during retries.

```python
import random
import time

def perform_operation(event):
    retries = 3
    for i in range(retries):
        try:
            # Perform operation
            return result
        except TransientError as e:
            logger.warning('Transient error occurred: %s', e)
            if i < retries - 1:
                delay = 2 ** i + random.random()
                time.sleep(delay)
            else:
                raise
```

5. Performance Profiling

Use performance profiling tools to identify bottlenecks and optimize the performance of your serverless functions. Tools like AWS X-Ray and New Relic provide insights into function execution times, resource utilization, and dependencies.

Best Practices for Debugging Serverless Applications

1. Instrumentation: Instrument your serverless applications with monitoring and observability tools to gain insights into their behavior and performance.

2. Version Control: Use version control to track changes to your serverless codebase and revert to previous versions if needed.

3. Automated Testing: Implement automated unit tests, integration tests, and end-to-end tests to catch bugs early and ensure the correctness of your serverless functions.

4. CI/CD Pipelines: Set up continuous integration and continuous deployment (CI/CD) pipelines to automate the testing and deployment of your serverless applications.

5. Code Reviews: Conduct code reviews to ensure that your serverless code adheres to best practices, is well-documented, and follows established patterns and conventions.

Debugging serverless applications requires a combination of techniques and tools tailored to the distributed and event-driven nature of serverless architectures. By using logging, remote debugging, local emulation, error handling, and performance profiling, you can effectively identify and fix issues in your serverless applications.

With a focus on best practices such as instrumentation, version control, automated testing, CI/CD pipelines, and code reviews, you can build and maintain reliable and scalable serverless applications that meet your business needs. Debugging is an integral part of the development process, and by adopting a proactive approach to debugging, you can ensure the stability and reliability of your serverless applications in production.

Advanced Debugging Strategies: Utilizing CloudWatch Logs, X-Ray Tracing, and Debugging Tools

Debugging serverless applications can be challenging due to their distributed nature and the lack of traditional development environments. However, with advanced debugging strategies and tools provided by AWS, you can effectively identify and troubleshoot issues in your serverless applications. In this article, we'll explore advanced debugging strategies utilizing AWS CloudWatch Logs, X-Ray Tracing, and other debugging tools, focusing on Python-based serverless applications developed with the Serverless Framework.

Understanding Advanced Debugging in Serverless Applications

Advanced debugging in serverless applications involves leveraging cloud-native tools and services to gain insights into the behavior and performance of your functions. Key components of advanced debugging include:

1. Logging: Utilizing detailed logging to capture application events and errors for analysis.

2. Tracing: Using distributed tracing to visualize the flow of requests across multiple services and identify bottlenecks.

3. Debugging Tools: Leveraging debugging tools provided by AWS to inspect the execution state of your functions and troubleshoot issues.

Utilizing CloudWatch Logs for Debugging

AWS CloudWatch Logs is a fully managed service for collecting, monitoring, and analyzing log data. It provides detailed insights into the behavior of your serverless applications, allowing you to identify and debug issues effectively.

Enabling CloudWatch Logs

To enable logging for your serverless functions, you can configure logging settings in the `serverless.yml` file:

```yaml
service: my-serverless-app

provider:
  name: aws
  runtime: python3.8
  stage: dev
  region: us-east-1
```

```
functions:
  myFunction:
    handler: handler.myFunction
    events:
      - http:
          path: mypath
          method: get
    # Enable logging
    logging:
      level: debug
      includePatterns: '*'
```
```

## Viewing Logs in CloudWatch Console

Once logging is enabled, you can view logs in the AWS CloudWatch Logs console. Logs are organized by log groups, with each function having its log group. You can filter logs based on specific keywords, time ranges, or log streams.

## Leveraging X-Ray Tracing for Distributed Debugging

AWS X-Ray is a distributed tracing service that allows you to trace requests as they travel through your
```

serverless application and identify performance bottlenecks and errors.

Instrumenting Your Application for X-Ray Tracing

To enable X-Ray tracing for your serverless functions, you can use the `AWS_XRAY_TRACING_ENABLED` environment variable:

```yaml
service: my-serverless-app

provider:
  name: aws
  runtime: python3.8
  stage: dev
  region: us-east-1

functions:
  myFunction:
    handler: handler.myFunction
    events:
      - http:
          path: mypath
          method: get
    # Enable X-Ray tracing
```

```
  environment:
    AWS_XRAY_TRACING_ENABLED: 'true'
```

Analyzing Traces in the X-Ray Console

Once tracing is enabled, you can view traces in the AWS X-Ray console. Traces provide a detailed view of the requests flowing through your serverless application, including information about the execution time, dependencies, and errors encountered.

Using Debugging Tools for Live Debugging

AWS provides several debugging tools that allow you to inspect the execution state of your serverless functions in real-time and troubleshoot issues as they occur.

AWS CloudWatch Debugger

The AWS CloudWatch Debugger is a feature that allows you to set up breakpoints in your code and capture snapshots of the execution state at runtime. You can use CloudWatch Debugger to diagnose issues, analyze variables, and understand the flow of execution.

AWS Lambda Insights

AWS Lambda Insights is a feature that provides enhanced monitoring and troubleshooting capabilities for Lambda functions. It collects additional performance metrics and logs for your functions, allowing you to diagnose performance issues and optimize resource utilization.

Best Practices for Advanced Debugging in Serverless Applications

1. Enable Detailed Logging: Configure detailed logging for your serverless functions to capture relevant information for debugging purposes.

2. Use X-Ray Tracing: Enable X-Ray tracing to visualize the flow of requests across your serverless application and identify performance bottlenecks.

3. Leverage Debugging Tools: Use AWS debugging tools such as CloudWatch Debugger and Lambda Insights to inspect the execution state of your functions in real-time.

4. Monitor Performance Metrics: Monitor performance metrics such as invocation count, duration, and error rate to identify trends and anomalies.

5. Implement Error Handling: Implement robust error handling and retry mechanisms in your functions to handle transient errors gracefully.

Advanced debugging in serverless applications requires a combination of techniques, tools, and best practices to effectively identify and troubleshoot issues. By utilizing AWS CloudWatch Logs, X-Ray Tracing, and other debugging tools provided by AWS, you can gain insights into the behavior and performance of your serverless applications and ensure their reliability and scalability in production.

With a proactive approach to debugging and monitoring, you can identify issues early, optimize performance, and deliver a seamless experience to your users. By following best practices and leveraging cloud-native debugging tools, you can build and maintain robust and reliable serverless applications that meet the needs of your business.

Chapter 9

Securing Your Serverless Functions: Authentication, Authorization, and Encryption

In the realm of serverless computing, where functions are ephemeral and auto-scalable, security becomes paramount. As the adoption of serverless architectures grows, so does the importance of securing serverless functions. In this guide, we'll explore best practices for securing serverless functions using authentication, authorization, and encryption, with a focus on the Python-based Serverless Framework.

Introduction to Serverless Security

Serverless computing abstracts away infrastructure management, allowing developers to focus solely on code. However, this abstraction introduces new security challenges, such as unauthorized access to functions, data breaches, and potential injection attacks. To mitigate these risks, a robust security strategy is essential.

Authentication

Authentication ensures that only authorized users or services can access serverless functions. One common method for authentication in serverless applications is JSON Web Tokens (JWT). Let's implement JWT-based authentication in a Python-based Serverless Framework application.

```python
# serverless.yml
service: secure-serverless

provider:
  name: aws
  runtime: python3.8

functions:
  hello:
    handler: handler.hello
    events:
      - http:
          path: hello
          method: get
          authorizer: jwtAuthorizer

resources:
```

```
Resources:
  JwtAuthorizer:
    Type: 'AWS::ApiGateway::Authorizer'
    Properties:
      AuthorizerResultTtlInSeconds: 300
      IdentitySource: method.request.header.Authorization
      Name: jwtAuthorizer
      RestApiId:
        Ref: ApiGatewayRestApi
      Type: token
```

```python
# handler.py
import json
import jwt

def hello(event, context):
    token = event['headers']['Authorization']
    try:
        payload = jwt.decode(token, 'your_secret_key', algorithms=['HS256'])
        return {
            "statusCode": 200,
            "body": json.dumps({
```

```
            "message": "Hello, " + payload['username'] +
"!"
        })
     }
   except jwt.ExpiredSignatureError:
      return {
         "statusCode": 401,
         "body": json.dumps({
            "error": "Token expired"
         })
      }
   except jwt.InvalidTokenError:
      return {
         "statusCode": 401,
         "body": json.dumps({
            "error": "Invalid token"
         })
      }
```

In this example, the `hello` function is protected by JWT authentication. The `handler` function decodes the JWT token and verifies it against a secret key.

Authorization

Authorization controls what authenticated users or services can do within the application. Role-Based Access Control (RBAC) is a common approach to authorization in serverless architectures. Let's extend our previous example to include RBAC.

```python
# handler.py
import json
import jwt

def hello(event, context):
    token = event['headers']['Authorization']
    try:
        payload = jwt.decode(token, 'your_secret_key', algorithms=['HS256'])
        if payload['role'] != 'admin':
            return {
                "statusCode": 403,
                "body": json.dumps({
                    "error": "Unauthorized"
                })
            }
        return {
            "statusCode": 200,
            "body": json.dumps({
```

```
            "message": "Hello, " + payload['username'] +
"!"
        })
    }
    except jwt.ExpiredSignatureError:
        return {
            "statusCode": 401,
            "body": json.dumps({
                "error": "Token expired"
            })
        }
    except jwt.InvalidTokenError:
        return {
            "statusCode": 401,
            "body": json.dumps({
                "error": "Invalid token"
            })
        }
```

In this updated `hello` function, we check the role of the user stored in the JWT payload. If the role is not "admin," we return a 403 Forbidden response.

Encryption

Encryption ensures that sensitive data is protected, both at rest and in transit. In serverless applications, data encryption is crucial, especially when dealing with personally identifiable information (PII) or sensitive business data. Let's encrypt data using AWS Key Management Service (KMS).

```python
import json
import boto3

def encrypt_data(data):
    kms = boto3.client('kms')
    response = kms.encrypt(
        KeyId='your_kms_key_id',
        Plaintext=data.encode()
    )
    encrypted_data = response['CiphertextBlob']
    return encrypted_data

def decrypt_data(encrypted_data):
    kms = boto3.client('kms')
    response = kms.decrypt(
        CiphertextBlob=encrypted_data
    )
    decrypted_data = response['Plaintext'].decode()
```

```
    return decrypted_data
```

In this example, `encrypt_data` and `decrypt_data` functions use AWS KMS to encrypt and decrypt data, respectively. Replace "your_kms_key_id" with your KMS key ID.

Securing serverless functions is a multifaceted task that requires a combination of authentication, authorization, and encryption. By implementing robust security measures, such as JWT-based authentication, RBAC, and data encryption with AWS KMS, you can mitigate security risks and build resilient serverless applications. Always stay updated with the latest security best practices and regularly review and audit your application's security posture to ensure ongoing protection against emerging threats.

Best Practices for Secure Development: Protecting Your Code, Data, and APIs

In today's interconnected digital landscape, secure development practices are more critical than ever. As developers embrace serverless architectures powered by frameworks like Python Serverless, ensuring the security of code, data, and APIs becomes paramount. In this guide, we'll delve into best practices for secure development, focusing on protecting your code, data, and APIs within a Python Serverless framework.

Securing Your Code

1. Code Reviews: Implement a robust code review process to catch security vulnerabilities early. Encourage peer reviews and utilize tools like static code analysis to identify potential security flaws.

2. Input Validation: Validate all input data to prevent injection attacks such as SQL injection, cross-site scripting (XSS), and command injection. Use libraries like `owasp-input-validator` to sanitize and validate user input.

```python
from owasp_input_validator import validate

def handler(event, context):
    # Validate input
    validated_data = validate(event['input'])
    # Proceed with validated data
```

3. Avoid Hardcoding Secrets: Never hardcode sensitive information like API keys or database credentials directly into your code. Utilize environment variables or a secure secrets manager to store and retrieve secrets dynamically.

```python
import os

api_key = os.environ.get('API_KEY')
```

Protecting Your Data

1. Encryption at Rest: Encrypt sensitive data stored in databases or file systems to protect it from unauthorized access. Leverage encryption libraries or cloud-native encryption services like AWS Key Management Service (KMS).

```python
import boto3

def encrypt_data(data):
    kms = boto3.client('kms')
```

```
response = kms.encrypt(
    KeyId='your_kms_key_id',
    Plaintext=data.encode()
)
encrypted_data = response['CiphertextBlob']
return encrypted_data
```
```

**2. Encryption in Transit:** Ensure that data transmitted over networks is encrypted using protocols like HTTPS. Use SSL/TLS certificates to secure communication between clients and servers.

**3. Data Minimization:** Only collect and store data that is necessary for your application's functionality. Minimizing data reduces the potential impact of a data breach and simplifies compliance with data protection regulations.

## Securing Your APIs

**1. API Gateway Authorization:** Implement fine-grained access control using API Gateway's built-in authorization mechanisms. Utilize API keys, Lambda authorizers, or OAuth 2.0 to authenticate and authorize requests.
```

```yaml
functions:
  hello:
    handler: handler.hello
    events:
      - http:
          path: hello
          method: get
          authorizer: aws_iam
```

2. Rate Limiting: Protect your APIs from abuse and denial-of-service (DoS) attacks by enforcing rate limits. Use API Gateway's rate limiting features or third-party services like AWS WAF (Web Application Firewall) to throttle incoming requests.

3. Input Validation and Sanitization: Apply input validation and sanitization techniques to API inputs to prevent injection attacks and data manipulation. Use frameworks like Flask or Django to automatically handle input validation.

```python
from flask import Flask, request
```

```
app = Flask(__name__)

@app.route('/submit', methods=['POST'])
def submit_form():
    username = request.form['username']
    password = request.form['password']
    # Validate and process inputs
```

Securing your code, data, and APIs is an ongoing process that requires diligence and proactive measures. By following best practices such as code reviews, input validation, encryption, and API security measures, you can mitigate the risk of security breaches and safeguard your applications against cyber threats. Stay informed about emerging security vulnerabilities and regularly update your security practices to adapt to evolving threats. Remember, security is everyone's responsibility, from developers to operations teams, and should be integrated into every stage of the development lifecycle.

Compliance Considerations: Building Secure Serverless Applications in Regulated Industries

In regulated industries such as finance, healthcare, and government, compliance with stringent security and privacy standards is non-negotiable. As organizations embrace serverless architectures powered by frameworks like Python Serverless, it's essential to ensure that these applications meet regulatory requirements. In this guide, we'll explore compliance considerations and best practices for building secure serverless applications in regulated industries.

Understanding Regulatory Compliance

1. HIPAA (Health Insurance Portability and Accountability Act): Healthcare organizations must comply with HIPAA regulations to ensure the security and privacy of patients' protected health information (PHI). This includes implementing technical safeguards, access controls, and encryption of PHI.

2. PCI DSS (Payment Card Industry Data Security Standard): Organizations that handle payment card data must adhere to PCI DSS standards to protect sensitive cardholder information. Compliance involves implementing secure network architectures, encryption, and regular security assessments.

3. GDPR (General Data Protection Regulation): GDPR mandates strict data protection requirements for organizations handling the personal data of European Union residents. Compliance involves obtaining explicit consent for data processing, implementing data encryption, and ensuring data subject rights.

Best Practices for Building Secure Serverless Applications in Regulated Industries

1. Data Encryption: Encrypt sensitive data at rest and in transit to protect it from unauthorized access. Utilize cloud-native encryption services like AWS Key Management Service (KMS) or Azure Key Vault for managing encryption keys securely.

```python
import boto3

def encrypt_data(data):
    kms = boto3.client('kms')
    response = kms.encrypt(
```

```
    KeyId='your_kms_key_id',
    Plaintext=data.encode()
)
encrypted_data = response['CiphertextBlob']
return encrypted_data
```

2. Access Control and Authentication: Implement strong authentication mechanisms to control access to serverless functions and data. Utilize identity and access management (IAM) policies, OAuth 2.0, or custom authorizers to authenticate and authorize users.

```yaml
functions:
  hello:
    handler: handler.hello
    events:
      - http:
          path: hello
          method: get
          authorizer: aws_iam
```

3. Audit Logging: Enable comprehensive audit logging to track access to sensitive data and serverless functions.

Log relevant events, including authentication attempts, data access, and configuration changes, to centralized logging platforms like AWS CloudWatch Logs or Azure Monitor.

```python
import logging

def handler(event, context):
    logger = logging.getLogger()
    logger.setLevel(logging.INFO)
    logger.info('Received event: %s', event)
```

4. Compliance Monitoring and Reporting: Regularly monitor and audit serverless applications for compliance with regulatory requirements. Use automated compliance scanning tools, perform vulnerability assessments, and maintain detailed compliance documentation for audits.

```python
import boto3

def compliance_scan():
    inspector = boto3.client('inspector')
    response = inspector.start_assessment_run(
```

```
        assessmentTemplateArn='your_assessment_template_ar
n'
    )
    return response['assessmentRunArn']
```

Implementing Compliance Controls in Python Serverless Framework

Let's demonstrate how to implement compliance controls in a Python Serverless application for a healthcare organization subject to HIPAA regulations.

```yaml
service: secure-healthcare-app

provider:
  name: aws
  runtime: python3.8

functions:
  hello:
    handler: handler.hello
    events:
      - http:
```

```
          path: hello
          method: get
          authorizer: aws_iam

resources:
  Resources:
    HelloFunctionRole:
      Type: AWS::IAM::Role
      Properties:
        RoleName: HelloFunctionRole
        AssumeRolePolicyDocument:
          Version: '2012-10-17'
          Statement:
            - Effect: Allow
              Principal:
                Service: lambda.amazonaws.com
              Action: sts:AssumeRole
        Policies:
          - PolicyName: HelloFunctionPolicy
            PolicyDocument:
              Version: '2012-10-17'
              Statement:
                - Effect: Allow
                  Action:
                    - logs:CreateLogGroup
                    - logs:CreateLogStream
```

```
      - logs:PutLogEvents
        Resource: 'arn:aws:logs:*:*:*'
      - Effect: Allow
        Action: kms:Decrypt
        Resource: 'your_kms_key_arn'
```

In this example, the `hello` function is protected by AWS IAM role-based authorization. Additionally, it has permissions to write logs to CloudWatch Logs and decrypt data using AWS KMS for encryption.

Building secure serverless applications in regulated industries requires careful consideration of compliance requirements and adherence to best practices. By implementing data encryption, access control, audit logging, and compliance monitoring, organizations can meet regulatory standards and protect sensitive data. It's crucial to continuously assess and improve the security posture of serverless applications to stay compliant with evolving regulations and mitigate security risks effectively. Remember, compliance is not a one-time effort but an ongoing commitment to maintaining the highest standards of security and privacy.

Chapter 10

Serverless on the Edge: Bringing Computing Closer to the Data with Lambda@Edge

In the era of distributed applications and content delivery networks (CDNs), the concept of serverless computing has evolved to include edge computing. With services like AWS Lambda@Edge, developers can execute serverless functions at edge locations closer to end-users, resulting in reduced latency and improved performance. In this guide, we'll explore Lambda@Edge and demonstrate how to leverage it within a Python Serverless framework to bring computing closer to the data.

Understanding Lambda@Edge

Lambda@Edge allows you to run serverless functions in response to CloudFront CDN events, such as viewer requests, origin responses, and cache behaviors. By deploying functions to edge locations worldwide, you can execute code closer to end-users, enabling dynamic content customization, security enforcement, and performance optimization.

Getting Started with Lambda@Edge

1. Set Up Your Serverless Framework Environment: Ensure you have the Serverless Framework installed and configured with your AWS credentials.

2. Create a New Serverless Project: Initialize a new Serverless project using the `create` command.

```bash
serverless create --template aws-python3 --name lambda-edge-project
```

3. Define Your Lambda@Edge Function: Create a new function in the `serverless.yml` file and specify the `events` trigger as `cloudFront`.

```yaml
service: lambda-edge-project

provider:
  name: aws
  runtime: python3.8

functions:
```

```yaml
edgeFunction:
  handler: handler.handler
  events:
    - cloudFront:
        eventType: viewer-request
        origin: my-cloudfront-distribution
```

Implementing Lambda@Edge Functions

Let's implement a simple Lambda@Edge function to add a custom header to incoming requests.

```python
# handler.py
def handler(event, context):
    request = event['Records'][0]['cf']['request']
    headers = request['headers']
    headers['custom-header'] = [{'key': 'Custom-Header', 'value': 'Serverless on the Edge'}]
    return request
```

Deploying Lambda@Edge Function

Deploy the Lambda@Edge function using the Serverless Framework.

```bash
serverless deploy
```

Use Cases for Lambda@Edge

1. Dynamic Content Customization: Modify responses based on viewer attributes such as geographic location, device type, or user preferences.

2. Security and Compliance: Enforce security policies, such as access control or content filtering, at the edge to protect origin servers from malicious traffic.

3. Performance Optimization: Cache control, image optimization, and content compression at edge locations can significantly improve page load times and reduce bandwidth costs.

Advanced Use Cases

1. A/B Testing: Distribute traffic between multiple origins or variations of content to conduct experiments and analyze user behavior.

2. Real-Time Analytics: Capture and process metrics or logs at edge locations for real-time monitoring and analysis of CDN traffic.

3. Bot Detection and Mitigation: Identify and block malicious bots or automated traffic patterns before they reach origin servers, reducing the risk of DDoS attacks and server overload.

Best Practices for Lambda@Edge

1. Optimize Cold Start Times: Minimize the size of your Lambda@Edge functions and reduce dependencies to improve cold start performance.

2. Monitor and Debug: Use CloudWatch Logs and metrics to monitor function execution and diagnose performance issues or errors.

3. Cost Optimization: Be mindful of invocation counts and data transfer costs associated with Lambda@Edge functions. Use caching and efficient code design to minimize overhead.

Lambda@Edge revolutionizes edge computing by bringing serverless capabilities to the edge of the network, closer to end-users. By leveraging Python Serverless framework, developers can seamlessly deploy and manage Lambda@Edge functions, unlocking new possibilities for dynamic content delivery, security enforcement, and performance optimization. As organizations continue to adopt distributed architectures and CDN-based solutions, Lambda@Edge emerges as a powerful tool for delivering faster, more personalized, and secure web experiences. Experiment with Lambda@Edge in your projects and explore the endless possibilities of serverless on the edge.

Serverless Machine Learning: Using Serverless Frameworks for AI/ML Workloads

In recent years, serverless computing has gained popularity for its ability to scale applications automatically and handle unpredictable workloads efficiently. This paradigm shift has extended to machine learning (ML) and artificial intelligence (AI) workloads, where serverless frameworks like Python Serverless offer a convenient and cost-effective way to deploy and manage AI models. In this guide, we'll explore how to leverage serverless frameworks for AI/ML workloads and demonstrate practical examples using Python Serverless.

Introduction to Serverless Machine Learning

Serverless machine learning combines the benefits of serverless computing with the power of machine learning algorithms, allowing developers to deploy and scale AI models without managing underlying infrastructure. With serverless frameworks, such as AWS Lambda or Azure Functions, you can run ML inference, data preprocessing, and model training tasks on demand, paying only for the resources consumed during execution.

Getting Started with Serverless Machine Learning

1. Setup Serverless Framework Environment: Install the Serverless Framework CLI and configure it with your cloud provider credentials (e.g., AWS, Azure).

2. Define Serverless Functions: Define serverless functions in a `serverless.yml` file, specifying the ML model code and dependencies.

```yaml
service: ml-serverless

provider:
  name: aws
  runtime: python3.8

functions:
  predictFunction:
    handler: handler.predict
```

3. Deploy Serverless Functions: Deploy the serverless functions to your cloud provider using the Serverless Framework CLI.

```bash
serverless deploy
```

Serverless Machine Learning Use Cases

1. Real-Time Predictions: Deploy ML models as serverless functions to make real-time predictions in response to incoming requests.

2. Data Processing Pipelines: Build serverless data processing pipelines for feature extraction, transformation, and batch inference on large datasets.

3. Anomaly Detection: Use serverless functions to detect anomalies in streaming data or time-series data, triggering alerts or actions as needed.

Example: Deploying a Sentiment Analysis Model

Let's deploy a simple sentiment analysis model using the Serverless Framework and AWS Lambda.

1. Define Sentiment Analysis Function:

```python
# handler.py
import boto3
import json

comprehend = boto3.client('comprehend')
```

```python
def predict(event, context):
    text = event['text']
    response = comprehend.detect_sentiment(Text=text, LanguageCode='en')
    sentiment = response['Sentiment']
    return {
        "statusCode": 200,
        "body": json.dumps({
            "sentiment": sentiment
        })
    }
```

2. Deploy Sentiment Analysis Function:

```yaml
# serverless.yml
service: ml-serverless

provider:
  name: aws
  runtime: python3.8

functions:
  predictFunction:
    handler: handler.predict
```

```

**3. Invoke Sentiment Analysis Function:**

```bash
serverless invoke --function predictFunction --data
'{"text": "This is a great tool!"}'
```

Best Practices for Serverless Machine Learning

1. Optimize Model Size: Minimize the size of ML models and dependencies to reduce cold start times and improve function performance.

2. Use Serverless Data Stores: Leverage serverless databases and storage services like AWS S3 or Azure Blob Storage for storing model artifacts and training data.

3. Monitor Performance: Monitor function execution times, memory usage, and invocation counts using cloud provider monitoring tools to optimize performance and identify bottlenecks.

Challenges and Considerations
```

1. Cold Start Latency: Serverless functions may experience cold starts, resulting in increased latency for the first invocation. Implement warm-up strategies or provisioned concurrency to mitigate cold start latency.

2. Resource Limits: Serverless functions have resource limits, such as memory and execution time. Ensure that ML models and data processing tasks fit within these limits to avoid function timeouts or resource exhaustion.

3. Cost Management: Monitor and optimize costs associated with serverless machine learning, including function invocations, memory usage, and cloud service fees. Consider reserved concurrency or usage-based pricing models for cost-effective scaling.

Serverless frameworks offer a compelling solution for deploying and managing machine learning workloads, enabling developers to focus on building AI/ML applications without worrying about infrastructure management. By leveraging Python Serverless framework and cloud provider services, you can deploy ML models as serverless functions, process data at scale, and make real-time predictions with ease. As serverless machine learning continues to evolve, it promises to democratize AI/ML development, making advanced analytics accessible to developers of all skill levels. Experiment with serverless machine learning in your projects and unlock the potential of AI-powered applications in the serverless era.

Continuous Integration and Delivery (CI/CD) for Serverless Applications

Continuous Integration and Delivery (CI/CD) practices are essential for modern software development, enabling teams to automate build, test, and deployment processes to deliver high-quality software rapidly. When it comes to serverless applications built using frameworks like Python Serverless, CI/CD pipelines play a crucial role in streamlining development workflows and ensuring smooth deployment to cloud environments. In this guide, we'll explore how to implement CI/CD for serverless applications using Python Serverless framework, along with best practices and practical examples.

Introduction to CI/CD for Serverless Applications

CI/CD for serverless applications involves automating the build, test, and deployment processes for serverless functions and resources. By setting up CI/CD pipelines, developers can integrate changes frequently, test them thoroughly, and deploy updates to production environments with confidence. Python Serverless framework provides a foundation for automating CI/CD workflows and integrating with popular CI/CD platforms such as GitHub Actions, Travis CI, or Jenkins.

Setting Up CI/CD with Python Serverless Framework

1. Setup Serverless Framework Environment: Install the Serverless Framework CLI and configure it with your cloud provider credentials (e.g., AWS, Azure).

2. Initialize a New Serverless Project: Create a new Serverless project using the `create` command.

```bash
serverless create --template aws-python3 --name my-serverless-app
```

3. Define Serverless Functions: Define serverless functions and resources in the `serverless.yml` file.

```yaml
service: my-serverless-app
```

```
provider:
  name: aws
  runtime: python3.8

functions:
  hello:
    handler: handler.hello
    events:
      - http:
          path: hello
          method: get
```

4. Set Up CI/CD Pipeline: Configure your CI/CD pipeline to build, test, and deploy serverless applications automatically.

Best Practices for CI/CD with Serverless Applications

1. Automated Testing: Implement automated tests for serverless functions and resources to ensure code quality and reliability. Include unit tests, integration tests, and end-to-end tests in your CI/CD pipeline.

2. Infrastructure as Code (IaC): Treat serverless infrastructure as code using tools like AWS CloudFormation or Azure Resource Manager templates. Define infrastructure configurations in version-controlled files to ensure consistency and reproducibility.

3. Environment Isolation: Use separate environments (e.g., development, staging, production) for testing and deployment to isolate changes and minimize the risk of introducing bugs or regressions.

4. Continuous Deployment: Automate deployment to production environments using continuous deployment pipelines. Leverage deployment strategies such as blue-green deployment or canary releases for safer and controlled rollouts.

Example CI/CD Pipeline for Serverless Applications

Let's create a simple CI/CD pipeline for a serverless application using GitHub Actions.

1. Define Workflow Configuration: Create a `.github/workflows/main.yml` file in your project repository with the following workflow configuration:

```yaml
name: CI/CD Pipeline

on:
  push:
    branches:
      - main

jobs:
  build:
    runs-on: ubuntu-latest

    steps:
      - name: Checkout code
        uses: actions/checkout@v2

      - name: Install dependencies
        run: npm install -g serverless && npm install

      - name: Deploy
        run: serverless deploy
        env:
          AWS_ACCESS_KEY_ID: ${{ secrets.AWS_ACCESS_KEY_ID }}
```

```
      AWS_SECRET_ACCESS_KEY: ${{
secrets.AWS_SECRET_ACCESS_KEY }}
```

2. Configure Secrets: Add AWS credentials as secrets in your GitHub repository settings to securely authenticate with your cloud provider.

3. Push Changes: Commit and push changes to your repository to trigger the CI/CD pipeline.

Monitoring and Feedback

1. Automated Alerts: Set up automated monitoring and alerting for serverless applications using cloud provider monitoring services (e.g., AWS CloudWatch, Azure Monitor) to detect and respond to performance issues or errors.

2. Pipeline Feedback: Collect and analyze feedback from CI/CD pipelines to identify bottlenecks, optimize build times, and improve deployment reliability. Utilize metrics and logs to track pipeline performance and success rates.

CI/CD practices are essential for accelerating the development and deployment of serverless applications, enabling teams to deliver features faster and with higher quality. By implementing CI/CD pipelines with Python Serverless framework, developers can automate build, test, and deployment processes, streamline development workflows, and ensure consistent and reliable deployments to cloud environments. As serverless adoption continues to grow, CI/CD will play a crucial role in driving innovation and agility in serverless application development. Experiment with CI/CD for your serverless projects and leverage the power of automation to deliver value to your users efficiently.

Serverless Microservices Architecture: Building Scalable and Agile Systems

Microservices architecture has gained popularity for its ability to break down monolithic applications into smaller, independent services, each with its own set of responsibilities. When combined with serverless computing, microservices architecture becomes even more powerful, allowing developers to build scalable, agile systems that can respond to changing demands efficiently. In this guide, we'll explore how to design and implement a serverless microservices architecture using

Python Serverless framework, along with best practices and practical examples.

Introduction to Serverless Microservices Architecture

Serverless microservices architecture combines the principles of microservices and serverless computing to create highly scalable, loosely coupled systems. Each microservice in the architecture is implemented as a serverless function, enabling automatic scaling, pay-per-execution pricing, and reduced operational overhead. Python Serverless framework provides the tools and infrastructure necessary to build and deploy serverless microservices seamlessly.

Design Principles for Serverless Microservices

1. Single Responsibility Principle (SRP): Each microservice should have a single responsibility or purpose, making it easier to manage, test, and scale independently.

2. Loose Coupling: Microservices should communicate with each other through well-defined APIs or messaging protocols, allowing them to evolve independently without affecting other services.

3. Resilience and Fault Tolerance: Design microservices to be resilient to failures by implementing retry mechanisms, circuit breakers, and graceful degradation strategies.

4. Event-Driven Architecture: Embrace event-driven architecture for asynchronous communication between microservices, enabling decoupled and scalable systems.

Building Serverless Microservices with Python Serverless Framework

1. Initialize a New Serverless Project: Create a new Serverless project for each microservice using the `create` command.

```bash
serverless create --template aws-python3 --name my-microservice
```

2. Define Microservice Function: Define the serverless function for the microservice in the `serverless.yml` file.

```yaml
service: my-microservice

provider:
  name: aws
  runtime: python3.8

functions:
  hello:
    handler: handler.hello
```

3. Implement Microservice Logic: Write the logic for the microservice function in the `handler.py` file.

```python
# handler.py
def hello(event, context):
    return {
        "statusCode": 200,
        "body": "Hello from my microservice!"
    }
```

4. Deploy Microservice: Deploy the microservice function to your cloud provider using the Serverless Framework CLI.

```bash
serverless deploy
```

Communication Between Microservices

1. HTTP REST APIs: Use HTTP REST APIs for synchronous communication between microservices, enabling request-response interactions.

2. Message Queues: Implement message queues or event streams (e.g., AWS SQS, Kafka) for asynchronous communication between microservices, allowing for decoupled and scalable architectures.

3. Event Sourcing: Embrace event sourcing patterns to capture and propagate domain events between microservices, enabling eventual consistency and auditability.

Best Practices for Serverless Microservices Architecture

1. Manage Dependencies: Minimize dependencies between microservices to avoid tight coupling and simplify deployment and scaling.

2. Service Discovery: Implement service discovery mechanisms (e.g., DNS, service registries) to enable dynamic discovery and routing of microservices.

3. Monitor and Observability: Utilize monitoring and observability tools to track the performance, health, and reliability of microservices in production environments.

4.Automated Testing: Implement automated testing for microservices to ensure functionality, reliability, and backward compatibility with each deployment.

Example: Building a Serverless Microservices Architecture

Let's build a simple serverless microservices architecture consisting of two microservices: `user` and `notification`.

1. Define Microservice Functions: Define the serverless functions for the `user` and `notification` microservices in separate Serverless projects.

2. Implement Microservice Logic: Implement the logic for each microservice function, including CRUD operations for users and notification processing.

3. Configure Communication: Use HTTP REST APIs or message queues to enable communication between the `user` and `notification` microservices.

4. Deploy Microservices: Deploy the microservices to your cloud provider using the Serverless Framework CLI.

<u>Challenges and Considerations</u>

1. Cold Start Latency: Serverless functions may experience cold starts, resulting in increased latency for the first invocation. Implement warm-up strategies or provisioned concurrency to mitigate cold start latency for critical microservices.

2. Distributed Tracing: Implement distributed tracing mechanisms (e.g., AWS X-Ray, Zipkin) to trace requests across microservices and diagnose performance issues in distributed systems.

3. Security: Implement security best practices, such as least privilege access controls, encryption in transit and at rest, and input validation, to protect sensitive data and prevent unauthorized access to microservices.

Serverless microservices architecture offers a scalable, agile approach to building modern applications, enabling developers to focus on business logic without worrying about infrastructure management. By leveraging Python Serverless framework, developers can design, deploy, and scale microservices effortlessly, creating flexible and resilient systems that can adapt to changing demands. Experiment with serverless microservices architecture in your projects and unlock the potential of serverless computing for building scalable, agile systems.

Chapter 11

Implementing Best Practices for Code Reusability, Efficiency, Maintainability, and Observability

Implementing best practices for code reusability, efficiency, maintainability, and observability is crucial for building robust and scalable applications. In this guide, we'll explore how to achieve these goals using Python and the Serverless framework.

Code Reusability:

Code reusability is essential for minimizing redundancy and maximizing efficiency in software development. One of the best practices for achieving code reusability is through modularization and the use of functions and classes.

```python
# Example of a reusable function
def add_numbers(a, b):
    return a + b

# Example of a reusable class
```

```
class Calculator:
    def add(self, a, b):
        return a + b
```

By encapsulating common functionalities into functions or classes, you can easily reuse them across your application.

Efficiency:

Efficiency in code refers to optimizing performance and resource utilization. This can be achieved through various techniques such as algorithm optimization, data structure selection, and minimizing resource consumption.

```python
# Example of using efficient data structures
from collections import defaultdict

# Using defaultdict for efficient storage of key-value pairs
data = defaultdict(int)
data['key'] += 1
```

Additionally, using asynchronous programming and concurrency can improve efficiency by allowing your application to perform multiple tasks simultaneously.

```python
# Example of asynchronous programming with asyncio
import asyncio

async def fetch_data(url):
    # Fetch data asynchronously
    ...

# Run multiple asynchronous tasks concurrently
async def main():
    await asyncio.gather(
        fetch_data('url1'),
        fetch_data('url2'),
        fetch_data('url3')
    )

asyncio.run(main())
```

Maintainability:

Maintainable code is easy to understand, modify, and extend. To ensure maintainability, follow coding standards, write clear and concise code, and document thoroughly.

```python
# Example of well-documented code
def calculate_area(radius):
    """
    Calculate the area of a circle.

    Args:
        radius (float): The radius of the circle.

    Returns:
        float: The area of the circle.
    """
    return 3.14 * radius**2
```

Additionally, adhere to design principles such as SOLID (Single Responsibility, Open/Closed, Liskov Substitution, Interface Segregation, Dependency Inversion) to create modular and extensible code.

Observability:

Observability is the ability to understand and monitor the internal state of a system. Implementing logging, metrics, and tracing is essential for gaining insights into the behavior of your application.

```python
# Example of logging
import logging

logging.basicConfig(level=logging.INFO)
logger = logging.getLogger(__name__)

def process_data(data):
    logger.info(f"Processing data: {data}")
    ...

# Example of metrics
from prometheus_client import Counter

requests_counter = Counter('requests_total', 'Total number of requests')

@handler
def handle_request(event, context):
    requests_counter.inc()
```

```
...

# Example of distributed tracing
from aws_xray_sdk.core import xray_recorder

@xray_recorder.capture('MyFunction')
def my_function():
    ...
```

By incorporating logging, metrics, and tracing into your application, you can effectively monitor its performance, diagnose issues, and optimize its behavior.

Serverless Framework:

The Serverless framework simplifies the deployment and management of serverless applications. It supports various cloud providers such as AWS, Azure, and Google Cloud Platform, allowing you to focus on writing code without worrying about infrastructure management.

```yaml
# Example of Serverless Framework configuration
service: my-service
```

```
provider:
  name: aws
  runtime: python3.8
  stage: dev
  region: us-east-1

functions:
  my_function:
    handler: handler.handle_request
    events:
      - http:
          path: my-function
          method: get
```

With the Serverless Framework, you can define your functions, their triggers, and other resources in a simple YAML configuration file, making it easy to deploy and manage your serverless applications.

By following these best practices and leveraging the Serverless framework, you can build scalable, efficient, maintainable, and observable applications with Python. Remember to continuously iterate and improve your codebase to meet the evolving needs of your users and business requirements.

Common Serverless Design Patterns: Strategies for Building Scalable and Reliable Applications

Common serverless design patterns are essential for building scalable and reliable applications using the Serverless framework. These patterns help developers address various challenges such as scalability, reliability, performance, and cost-effectiveness. Let's explore some of the most common serverless design patterns with examples in Python using the Serverless framework.

1. Function-as-a-Service (FaaS):

FaaS is the foundation of serverless computing, allowing developers to deploy individual functions that are triggered by events.

```yaml
# Example of defining a function in Serverless framework
service: my-service
```

```
provider:
  name: aws
  runtime: python3.8
  stage: dev
  region: us-east-1

functions:
  my_function:
    handler: handler.handle_request
    events:
      - http:
          path: my-function
          method: get
```

In this example, `my_function` is a serverless function that will be triggered by an HTTP GET request.

2. Event-Driven Architecture:

Event-driven architecture is a design pattern where components within an application communicate asynchronously through events.

```python
# Example of an event-driven function in Python
```

```python
import json

def process_event(event, context):
    # Process the event data
    data = json.loads(event['body'])
    ...

# Trigger the function with an event
event = {
    'body': '{"key": "value"}'
}
process_event(event, None)
```

In this example, `process_event` is an event-driven function that processes event data, which can be triggered by various event sources such as HTTP requests, message queues, or database changes.

3. Asynchronous Processing:

Asynchronous processing allows long-running tasks to be executed outside the request-response cycle, improving performance and scalability.

```python
```

```
# Example of asynchronous processing using asyncio
import asyncio

async def process_task():
    # Perform time-consuming task asynchronously
    await asyncio.sleep(5)
    ...

# Trigger the asynchronous task
async def main():
    await process_task()

asyncio.run(main())
```

In this example, `process_task` is an asynchronous function that performs a time-consuming task asynchronously, allowing the main program to continue execution without waiting for the task to complete.

4. Stream Processing:

Stream processing is a design pattern for processing continuous streams of data, commonly used for real-time analytics and event processing.

```python
# Example of stream processing using AWS Kinesis
import boto3

kinesis = boto3.client('kinesis')

def process_record(record):
    # Process individual records from the stream
    ...

# Process records from the Kinesis stream
response = kinesis.get_records(StreamName='my-stream', Limit=10)
for record in response['Records']:
    process_record(record)
```

In this example, `process_record` is a function that processes individual records from an AWS Kinesis stream, allowing you to perform real-time analytics on the streaming data.

5. Orchestration:

Orchestration is the coordination of multiple serverless functions or services to accomplish complex workflows.

```python
# Example of orchestrating multiple functions
import json

def step1(event, context):
    # Perform step 1 of the workflow
    ...

def step2(event, context):
    # Perform step 2 of the workflow
    ...

def orchestrate_workflow(event, context):
    # Orchestrate the workflow by invoking step functions
    step1_result = step1(event, context)
    step2_result = step2(step1_result, context)
    return step2_result
```

In this example, `orchestrate_workflow` orchestrates the execution of multiple functions (`step1` and `step2`) to accomplish a complex workflow.

6. Caching:

Caching is a technique for storing frequently accessed data in memory to improve performance and reduce latency.

```python
# Example of caching using AWS Lambda cache
import json
import boto3

dynamodb = boto3.client('dynamodb')

def get_data_from_cache(key):
    # Retrieve data from cache
    ...

def fetch_data_from_source(key):
    # Fetch data from the data source
    ...

def get_data(event, context):
    key = event['queryStringParameters']['key']
    data = get_data_from_cache(key)
    if not data:
        data = fetch_data_from_source(key)
        # Store data in cache for future use
        ...
```

```
    return {
        'statusCode': 200,
        'body': json.dumps(data)
    }
```

In this example, `get_data` retrieves data from a cache, and if the data is not found in the cache, it fetches it from the data source and stores it in the cache for future use.

By leveraging these common serverless design patterns and the Serverless framework, you can build scalable, reliable, and cost-effective applications that efficiently handle various use cases and workloads. Whether you're processing events, orchestrating workflows, or optimizing performance with caching, understanding and applying these patterns will help you architect robust serverless applications in Python. Remember to consider factors such as scalability, reliability, performance, and cost when designing and implementing your serverless solutions.

Advanced Error Handling and State Management Techniques in Serverless Functions

Advanced error handling and state management techniques are essential for building robust and reliable serverless functions. In this guide, we'll explore various strategies and best practices for handling errors and managing state in serverless functions using Python and the Serverless framework.

Error Handling:

Error handling is crucial for gracefully handling exceptions and failures in serverless functions. Here are some advanced error handling techniques:

1. Custom Error Handling Middleware:

Implement custom error handling middleware to centralize error handling logic and improve code maintainability.

```python
# Example of custom error handling middleware in Python
```

```python
def error_handler_middleware(handler):
    def wrapper(event, context):
        try:
            return handler(event, context)
        except Exception as e:
            # Handle the exception
            return {
                'statusCode': 500,
                'body': 'Internal Server Error'
            }
    return wrapper

# Apply the middleware to the function handler
@error_handler_middleware
def my_function(event, context):
    # Function logic
    ...
```

In this example, `error_handler_middleware` is a custom middleware that wraps the function handler and catches any exceptions, allowing you to handle errors centrally.

2. Structured Logging:

Use structured logging to capture detailed information about errors, including stack traces, timestamps, and contextual data.

```python
# Example of structured logging in Python
import logging

logger = logging.getLogger(__name__)

def my_function(event, context):
    try:
        # Function logic
        ...
    except Exception as e:
        # Log the exception with detailed information
        logger.error('An error occurred', exc_info=True, extra={'event': event, 'context': context})
        return {
            'statusCode': 500,
            'body': 'Internal Server Error'
        }
```

In this example, `logger.error` logs the exception with additional contextual information such as the event and context objects, facilitating easier debugging and troubleshooting.

State Management:

State management is critical for maintaining the state of serverless functions across invocations and handling stateful workflows. Here are some advanced state management techniques:

1. External State Storage:

Use external storage services such as databases or object storage to persist and manage state across function invocations.

```python
# Example of using DynamoDB for state management
import boto3

dynamodb = boto3.resource('dynamodb')
table = dynamodb.Table('my_table')

def my_function(event, context):
    # Retrieve state from DynamoDB
    state = table.get_item(Key={'id': 'my_id'})['Item']
```

```python
    # Update state
    state['count'] += 1
    table.put_item(Item=state)

    # Function logic
    ...
```

In this example, DynamoDB is used to store and manage the state of the function across invocations, ensuring consistency and durability.

2. Idempotent Operations:

Design functions to be idempotent, meaning that performing the same operation multiple times produces the same result.

```python
# Example of idempotent operation with DynamoDB
def my_function(event, context):
    try:
        # Perform idempotent operation
        dynamodb.put_item(Item={'id': 'my_id', 'data': 'value'}, ConditionExpression='attribute_not_exists(id)')
```

```
    except dynamodb.meta.client.exceptions.ConditionalCheckFailedException:
        # Ignore if the item already exists
        pass

    # Function logic
    ...
```

In this example, `put_item` operation is designed to be idempotent by using a conditional expression to ensure that the item is only inserted if it doesn't already exist.

3. State Machine Orchestration:

Use state machines to orchestrate complex workflows and manage state transitions across multiple functions.

```yaml
# Example of defining a state machine with AWS Step Functions
{
  "Comment": "A simple state machine example",
  "StartAt": "ProcessData",
  "States": {
```

```
    "ProcessData": {
      "Type": "Task",
      "Resource": "arn:aws:lambda:REGION:ACCOUNT_ID:function:ProcessDataFunction",
      "Next": "SendNotification"
    },
    "SendNotification": {
      "Type": "Task",
      "Resource": "arn:aws:lambda:REGION:ACCOUNT_ID:function:SendNotificationFunction",
      "End": true
    }
  }
```

In this example, AWS Step Functions is used to define a state machine that orchestrates the execution of two functions (`ProcessDataFunction` and `SendNotificationFunction`) in a sequential manner.

By implementing advanced error handling and state management techniques in serverless functions, you can enhance the reliability, scalability, and maintainability of your serverless applications. Whether you're handling exceptions gracefully, persisting state across invocations, or orchestrating complex workflows with state machines, understanding and applying these techniques will help you build robust and resilient serverless architectures. Remember to consider factors such as fault tolerance, consistency, and performance when designing and implementing error handling and state management strategies for your serverless functions.

Chapter 12

Building real-time applications with WebSockets and serverless.

Building real-time applications with WebSockets and serverless architecture offers a powerful solution for creating interactive and dynamic experiences. In this guide, we'll explore how to implement real-time features using WebSockets with Python and the Serverless Framework.

Understanding WebSockets:

WebSockets provide a full-duplex communication channel over a single TCP connection, enabling real-time, bi-directional communication between clients and servers. Unlike traditional HTTP requests, which are stateless and require multiple connections for communication, WebSockets maintain a persistent connection, allowing for efficient real-time data exchange.

1. Setting Up a WebSocket Server with Serverless:

We'll use the Serverless Framework to deploy a WebSocket server using AWS API Gateway and AWS Lambda.

a. Install Serverless Framework:

First, install the Serverless Framework using npm:

```bash
npm install -g serverless
```

b. Create a New Serverless Project:

Create a new directory for your project and navigate into it:

```bash
mkdir websocket-demo
cd websocket-demo
```

Initialize a new Serverless project:

```bash
```

```
serverless create --template aws-python3 --name websocket-demo
```

c. Implement WebSocket Handler:

Create a Python function to handle WebSocket connections and messages:

```python
# handler.py

import json

def connect(event, context):
    return {
        'statusCode': 200,
        'body': json.dumps({
            'message': 'Connected successfully.'
        })
    }

def disconnect(event, context):
    return {
        'statusCode': 200,
        'body': json.dumps({
```

```
            'message': 'Disconnected successfully.'
        })
    }

def default(event, context):
    return {
        'statusCode': 200,
        'body': json.dumps({
            'message': 'Received message: ' + event['body']
        })
    }
```

d. Configure WebSocket Routes:

Define WebSocket routes in your `serverless.yml` configuration:

```yaml
# serverless.yml

service: websocket-demo

provider:
  name: aws
  runtime: python3.8
```

```
functions:
  connect:
    handler: handler.connect
    events:
      - websocket: $connect
  disconnect:
    handler: handler.disconnect
    events:
      - websocket: $disconnect
  default:
    handler: handler.default
    events:
      - websocket: $default
```

e. Deploy WebSocket Server:

Deploy your WebSocket server using the Serverless Framework:

```bash
serverless deploy
```

2. Building a Real-Time Application:

Now that we have our WebSocket server deployed, let's build a simple real-time chat application using HTML, JavaScript, and the WebSocket API.

a. HTML Structure:

Create an HTML file (`index.html`) with a simple chat interface:

```html
<!-- index.html -->

<!DOCTYPE html>
<html lang="en">
<head>
    <meta charset="UTF-8">
    <meta name="viewport" content="width=device-width, initial-scale=1.0">
    <title>Real-Time Chat</title>
</head>
<body>
    <div id="chat">
        <textarea id="messages" rows="10" cols="50" readonly></textarea>
```

```
        <input type="text" id="inputMessage"
placeholder="Type your message...">
            <button onclick="sendMessage()">Send</button>
        </div>

        <script src="client.js"></script>
</body>
</html>
```

b. JavaScript Client:

Implement JavaScript code (`client.js`) to connect to the WebSocket server and send/receive messages:

```javascript
// client.js

const websocketUrl = '<YOUR_WEBSOCKET_URL>';
// Replace with your WebSocket URL

const socket = new WebSocket(websocketUrl);

socket.onopen = () => {
    console.log('Connected to WebSocket server');
};
```

```
socket.onmessage = (event) => {
  const message = JSON.parse(event.data);
  displayMessage(message);
};

function sendMessage() {
  const inputMessage = document.getElementById('inputMessage').value;
  socket.send(inputMessage);
}

function displayMessage(message) {
  const messagesTextArea = document.getElementById('messages');
  messagesTextArea.value += message + '\n';
}
```

By combining WebSockets with serverless architecture, you can build real-time applications that offer seamless communication and interactive experiences for users. With the Serverless Framework, deploying WebSocket servers becomes straightforward, allowing you to focus on building the core functionality of your real-time applications. Whether it's a chat application, a collaborative editing tool, or a live data dashboard, the combination of WebSockets and serverless opens up a wide range of possibilities for building modern, real-time applications.

Implementing GraphQL APIs in a serverless architecture.

Implementing GraphQL APIs in a serverless architecture offers a flexible and scalable approach to building modern web applications. GraphQL enables clients to query and manipulate data with a single endpoint, providing greater flexibility and efficiency compared to traditional REST APIs. In this guide, we'll explore how to implement GraphQL APIs using Python and the Serverless Framework.

Understanding GraphQL:

GraphQL is a query language for APIs that enables clients to request only the data they need, allowing for more efficient data fetching and reduced network overhead. With GraphQL, clients can specify the structure of the data they require, eliminating over-fetching and under-fetching of data commonly associated with REST APIs.

1. Setting Up a Serverless Project:

We'll use the Serverless Framework to deploy a GraphQL API using AWS AppSync, AWS Lambda, and Amazon DynamoDB.

a. Install Serverless Framework:

If you haven't already, install the Serverless Framework:

```bash
npm install -g serverless
```

b. Create a New Serverless Project:

Create a new directory for your project and navigate into it:

```bash
mkdir graphql-api
cd graphql-api
```

Initialize a new Serverless project:

```bash
serverless create --template aws-python3 --name graphql-api
```

2. Implementing a GraphQL Schema:

Create a GraphQL schema definition file (`schema.graphql`) to define the structure of your API:

```graphql
# schema.graphql

type Query {
  getTodos: [Todo!]!
}

type Mutation {
  createTodo(input: TodoInput!): Todo
}

type Todo {
  id: ID!
```

```
  title: String!
  completed: Boolean!
}

input TodoInput {
  title: String!
  completed: Boolean!
}
```

3. Implementing Resolver Functions:

Define resolver functions to handle GraphQL queries and mutations:

```python
# handler.py

import json

def getTodos(event, context):
    todos = [...]  # Retrieve todos from database
    return {
        'statusCode': 200,
        'body': json.dumps(todos)
    }
```

```
def createTodo(event, context):
    data = json.loads(event['body'])
    # Save todo to database
    return {
        'statusCode': 201,
        'body': json.dumps(data)
    }
```

4. Configuring AWS AppSync:

Configure AWS AppSync to create a GraphQL API with the Serverless Framework:

```yaml
# serverless.yml

service: graphql-api

provider:
  name: aws
  runtime: python3.8

functions:
  getTodos:
```

```
    handler: handler.getTodos
    events:
      - http:
          path: getTodos
          method: get
  createTodo:
    handler: handler.createTodo
    events:
      - http:
          path: createTodo
          method: post

resources:
  Resources:
    GraphQLAPI:
      Type: AWS::AppSync::GraphQLApi
      Properties:
        Name: TodoApp
        AuthenticationType: API_KEY
        UserPoolConfig:
          AwsRegion: ${self:provider.region}
          DefaultAction: ALLOW
```

5. Deploying the GraphQL API:

Deploy your GraphQL API using the Serverless Framework:

```bash
serverless deploy
```

Implementing GraphQL APIs in a serverless architecture using Python and the Serverless Framework offers a powerful solution for building flexible and scalable web applications. With GraphQL, clients can efficiently query and manipulate data using a single endpoint, reducing network overhead and improving performance. By leveraging serverless technologies such as AWS AppSync, AWS Lambda, and Amazon DynamoDB, you can build and deploy GraphQL APIs with ease, focusing on delivering value to your users without worrying about infrastructure management. Whether it's a simple todo application or a complex data-driven platform, GraphQL and serverless architecture provide the foundation for building modern, scalable, and efficient web applications.

Using serverless for machine learning model deployment.

Deploying machine learning models with serverless architecture offers a scalable and cost-effective solution for serving predictions to users or applications. In this guide, we'll explore how to use Python, the Serverless Framework, and AWS Lambda to deploy machine learning models in a serverless environment.

Understanding Serverless for Machine Learning Deployment:

Serverless architecture abstracts away infrastructure management, allowing developers to focus on building and deploying applications without worrying about server provisioning or scaling. By leveraging serverless platforms like AWS Lambda, you can deploy machine learning models as serverless functions, enabling on-demand execution and automatic scaling based on incoming requests.

1. Preparing Your Machine Learning Model:

Before deploying your machine learning model, you need to prepare it for inference. This involves training the model using your dataset and saving it in a format suitable for deployment. Let's assume you have already trained a machine learning model using scikit-learn and saved it as a `.pkl` file.

Example:

```python
# Train and save a machine learning model using scikit-learn
import pickle
from sklearn.ensemble import RandomForestClassifier
from sklearn.datasets import load_iris

# Load dataset
iris = load_iris()
X, y = iris.data, iris.target

# Train model
model = RandomForestClassifier()
model.fit(X, y)

# Save model
with open('model.pkl', 'wb') as f:
    pickle.dump(model, f)
```

2. Creating a Serverless Function for Inference:

Now, let's create a serverless function using AWS Lambda to perform inference with our machine learning model. We'll use the Serverless Framework to deploy the function to AWS Lambda.

a. Install Serverless Framework:

If you haven't already, install the Serverless Framework:

```bash
npm install -g serverless
```

b. Create a New Serverless Project:

Create a new directory for your project and navigate into it:

```bash
mkdir ml-model-deployment
cd ml-model-deployment
```

Initialize a new Serverless project:

```bash
serverless create --template aws-python3 --name ml-model
```

c. Implement the Inference Function:

Create a Python file (`handler.py`) to implement the inference function:

```python
# handler.py

import pickle
import json
import numpy as np

# Load the trained model
with open('model.pkl', 'rb') as f:
    model = pickle.load(f)

def predict(event, context):
    # Parse input data
    data = json.loads(event['body'])
    features = np.array(data['features']).reshape(1, -1)
```

```
# Perform inference
prediction = model.predict(features).tolist()

# Return prediction
return {
   'statusCode': 200,
   'body': json.dumps({
      'prediction': prediction
   })
}
```

d. Configure Serverless Framework:

Define the serverless function in your `serverless.yml` configuration file:

```yaml
# serverless.yml

service: ml-model

provider:
  name: aws
  runtime: python3.8
```

```
functions:
  predict:
    handler: handler.predict
    events:
      - http:
          path: predict
          method: post
```

3. Deploying the Machine Learning Model:

Deploy your machine learning model as a serverless function using the Serverless Framework:

```bash
serverless deploy
```

4. Testing the Deployment:

Test the deployed function by sending HTTP POST requests with sample input data to the endpoint:

```bash
curl -X POST https://your-api-gateway-url.amazonaws.com/dev/predict \
```

```
-H "Content-Type: application/json" \
-d '{"features": [5.1, 3.5, 1.4, 0.2]}'
```

Deploying machine learning models with serverless architecture using Python and the Serverless Framework offers a convenient and scalable solution for serving predictions in production environments. By leveraging serverless platforms like AWS Lambda, you can deploy models as serverless functions, enabling automatic scaling, on-demand execution, and cost-effective deployment. Whether it's for real-time predictions in web applications, batch processing of data, or integration with other services, serverless machine learning deployment provides a flexible and efficient solution for deploying machine learning models at scale.

Handling multi-region deployments and global applications.

Handling multi-region deployments and global applications with serverless architecture is crucial for ensuring high availability, low latency, and fault tolerance across different geographic regions. In this guide, we'll explore how to deploy serverless applications to multiple regions using the Serverless Framework and Python.

Understanding Multi-Region Deployments:

Multi-region deployments involve replicating serverless applications across multiple geographic regions to distribute traffic, improve performance, and mitigate the risk of downtime. By deploying serverless functions to multiple regions, you can ensure that users from different parts of the world have low-latency access to your application and that your application remains available even in the event of regional outages.

1. Setting Up Multi-Region Deployment:

We'll use the Serverless Framework to deploy a simple serverless application to multiple AWS regions.

a. Install Serverless Framework:

If you haven't already, install the Serverless Framework:

```bash
npm install -g serverless
```

b. Create a New Serverless Project:

Create a new directory for your project and navigate into it:

```bash
mkdir multi-region-app
cd multi-region-app
```

Initialize a new Serverless project:

```bash
serverless create --template aws-python3 --name multi-region-app
```

2. Implementing a Simple Serverless Function:

Let's implement a simple serverless function that returns the current region.

a. Implement Serverless Function:

Create a Python file (`handler.py`) to implement the serverless function:

```python
# handler.py

import json
import os

def get_region(event, context):
    region = os.environ.get('AWS_REGION', 'unknown')
    return {
        'statusCode': 200,
        'body': json.dumps({
            'region': region
        })
    }
```

b. Configure Serverless Framework:

Define the serverless function in your `serverless.yml` configuration file:

```yaml
# serverless.yml
```

```
service: multi-region-app

provider:
  name: aws
  runtime: python3.8

functions:
  getRegion:
    handler: handler.get_region
    events:
      - http:
          path: region
          method: get
```

3. Deploying to Multiple Regions:

Now, let's deploy the serverless application to multiple AWS regions using the Serverless Framework.

a. Update Serverless Configuration:

Add custom configuration to your `serverless.yml` file to specify the regions you want to deploy to:

```yaml
# serverless.yml

service: multi-region-app

provider:
  name: aws
  runtime: python3.8
  region: us-east-1  # Default region for deployment

functions:
  getRegion:
    handler: handler.get_region
    events:
      - http:
          path: region
          method: get

custom:
  regions:
    - us-west-2
    - eu-west-1
```

b. Deploy to Multiple Regions:

Deploy the serverless application to multiple regions using the Serverless Framework:

```bash
serverless deploy --region <region-name>
```

4. Testing the Deployment:

Test the deployed application by sending HTTP GET requests to the endpoints in different regions:

```bash
curl https://<api-gateway-url>.execute-api.<region>.amazonaws.com/dev/region
```

Handling multi-region deployments and global applications with serverless architecture using the Serverless Framework provides a scalable and resilient solution for ensuring high availability and low latency across different geographic regions. By deploying serverless functions to multiple regions, you can distribute traffic, improve performance, and mitigate the risk of downtime caused by regional outages. Whether it's for serving global users, achieving regulatory compliance, or improving disaster recovery capabilities, multi-region deployments offer a robust and cost-effective approach for building and deploying serverless applications at scale.

Chapter 13

Case Studies and Real-World Examples

Detailed case studies of successful serverless implementations.

Case Study: E-Commerce Recommendation System

A large e-commerce company, let's call it "E-Shop", wanted to enhance its customer experience by providing personalized product recommendations to users. The traditional approach involved maintaining a monolithic system that struggled to scale during peak times and incurred high operational costs. To address these challenges, E-Shop decided to adopt a serverless architecture leveraging AWS Lambda and the Serverless Framework. Python was chosen as the primary programming language due to its simplicity and wide adoption within the company's engineering team.

Architecture Overview:

The serverless architecture consisted of several AWS services orchestrated using the Serverless Framework:

1. AWS Lambda: Used to run the recommendation engine logic. Each recommendation request triggers a Lambda function invocation.

2. Amazon DynamoDB: A NoSQL database used to store user profiles, purchase history, and product metadata.

3. Amazon S3: Used to store static assets such as product images and HTML templates for email recommendations.

4. Amazon API Gateway: Provides a RESTful API to interact with the recommendation system.

5. Amazon CloudWatch: Monitors and logs system events for debugging and performance analysis.

Implementation Details:

1. User Profile Management (Lambda + DynamoDB):

When a user registers or logs in, a Lambda function is triggered to update or retrieve their profile information from DynamoDB. This function is responsible for managing user preferences, purchase history, and other relevant data.

```python
import boto3

dynamodb = boto3.resource('dynamodb')
table = dynamodb.Table('user_profiles')

def update_profile(event, context):
    user_id = event['user_id']
    preferences = event['preferences']
    purchase_history = event['purchase_history']

    table.put_item(
        Item={
            'user_id': user_id,
            'preferences': preferences,
            'purchase_history': purchase_history
        }
    )
    return {
        'statusCode': 200,
        'body': 'Profile updated successfully'
    }

def get_profile(event, context):
```

```python
    user_id = event['user_id']

    response = table.get_item(
        Key={
            'user_id': user_id
        }
    )
    return {
        'statusCode': 200,
        'body': response['Item']
    }
```

2. Recommendation Engine (Lambda):

Upon receiving a recommendation request, a Lambda function processes the user's profile and generates personalized recommendations based on their preferences and purchase history.

```python
import boto3

dynamodb = boto3.resource('dynamodb')
products_table = dynamodb.Table('products')

def recommend_products(event, context):
```

```
    user_id = event['user_id']
    # Retrieve user profile from DynamoDB
    user_profile = get_user_profile(user_id)
    # Implement recommendation logic based on user
profile
    recommended_products = recommend(user_profile)
    return {
        'statusCode': 200,
        'body': recommended_products
    }

def get_user_profile(user_id):
    # Retrieve user profile from DynamoDB
    pass

def recommend(user_profile):
    # Implement recommendation logic
    pass
```

3. API Integration (API Gateway):

API Gateway is configured to trigger Lambda functions based on incoming HTTP requests. Endpoints are defined to interact with the recommendation system, such as retrieving user profiles and fetching product recommendations.

```yaml
service: e-commerce-recommendations

provider:
  name: aws
  runtime: python3.8

functions:
  updateProfile:
    handler: handler.update_profile
    events:
      - http:
          path: profile
          method: post
  getProfile:
    handler: handler.get_profile
    events:
      - http:
          path: profile/{user_id}
          method: get
  recommendProducts:
    handler: handler.recommend_products
    events:
```

```
    - http:
        path: recommendations
        method: post
```

Benefits:

1. Scalability: The serverless architecture automatically scales to handle varying workloads, ensuring consistent performance during peak times.

2. Cost-Efficiency: E-Shop significantly reduces operational costs by paying only for the compute resources consumed by Lambda functions, rather than maintaining a fleet of always-on servers.

3. Developer Productivity: The Serverless Framework abstracts away infrastructure management, allowing developers to focus on writing business logic and delivering features faster.

4. Flexibility: By leveraging AWS services like DynamoDB and S3, E-Shop can easily adapt the recommendation system to evolving business requirements without worrying about infrastructure provisioning.

Through the adoption of a serverless architecture powered by the Serverless Framework and Python, E-Shop successfully implemented a scalable and cost-effective recommendation system, enhancing the overall customer experience and driving business growth. This case study demonstrates the effectiveness of serverless computing in modernizing traditional applications and achieving agility in the rapidly evolving e-commerce landscape.

Lessons learned from real-world projects.

1. Embrace Event-Driven Architecture:

In serverless applications, functions are triggered by events from various sources such as HTTP requests, database changes, file uploads, and scheduled tasks. Embracing event-driven architecture allows for a decoupled and scalable system where each function performs a specific task in response to events.

```python
import boto3

def process_event(event, context):
```

```
    # Handle event logic
    pass
```

2. Optimize Function Performance:

Serverless functions have cold start times, which can impact response latency for infrequently used functions. To mitigate this, optimize function performance by minimizing dependencies, using lightweight frameworks, and implementing efficient code practices.

```python
import json

def lambda_handler(event, context):
    # Process event
    return {
        'statusCode': 200,
        'body': json.dumps('Function executed successfully')
    }
```

3. Leverage Managed Services:

Utilize managed services provided by cloud providers to offload operational tasks such as database management, authentication, and file storage. This reduces maintenance overhead and allows developers to focus on application logic.

```python
import boto3

dynamodb = boto3.resource('dynamodb')
table = dynamodb.Table('example_table')

def get_item(item_id):
    response = table.get_item(Key={'id': item_id})
    return response['Item']
```

4. Implement Error Handling and Monitoring:

Serverless applications require robust error handling mechanisms to handle failures gracefully and prevent cascading errors. Use logging and monitoring tools to track function invocations, identify performance bottlenecks, and troubleshoot issues effectively.

```python
```

```
import logging

logger = logging.getLogger()
logger.setLevel(logging.INFO)

def lambda_handler(event, context):
   try:
      # Process event
      return {
         'statusCode': 200,
         'body': 'Function executed successfully'
      }
   except Exception as e:
      logger.error(f'Error: {str(e)}')
      return {
         'statusCode': 500,
         'body': 'Internal Server Error'
      }
```

5. Secure Function Environments:

Ensure secure configuration and access control for serverless functions by following best practices such as least privilege access, encryption of sensitive data, and implementing authentication and authorization mechanisms.

```python
import boto3

client = boto3.client('secretsmanager')

def get_secret(secret_name):
    response = client.get_secret_value(SecretId=secret_name)
    return response['SecretString']
```

6. Plan for Vendor Lock-In:

While serverless offers scalability and cost-effectiveness, it's essential to consider the implications of vendor lock-in. Design applications with portability in mind by using vendor-agnostic tools and adhering to cloud-agnostic patterns where possible.

```yaml
service: example-service

provider:
```

```
name: aws
runtime: python3.8
region: us-east-1
```

7. Test Locally and Automate Deployment:

Facilitate rapid development cycles by testing serverless functions locally using emulators and automated testing frameworks. Implement CI/CD pipelines to automate deployment, testing, and monitoring workflows for seamless integration and delivery.

```bash
$ serverless invoke local -f function_name
```

8. Monitor and Optimize Costs:

Monitor resource usage, analyze billing metrics, and implement cost optimization strategies such as resource pooling, auto-scaling, and using reserved instances to minimize operational costs and maximize ROI.

```yaml
provider:
```

```
  name: aws
  environment:
    DYNAMODB_TABLE: ${self:service}-table-${opt:stage, self:provider.stage}
```

By embracing event-driven architecture, optimizing performance, leveraging managed services, implementing robust error handling, ensuring security, planning for vendor lock-in, testing locally, automating deployment, and monitoring costs, organizations can successfully navigate the complexities of real-world serverless projects. These lessons learned provide valuable insights for building scalable, resilient, and cost-effective applications using the Serverless Framework with Python.

Practical examples of common serverless use cases, such as chatbots, image processing, and IoT.

let's explore practical examples of common serverless use cases including chatbots, image processing, and IoT using the Serverless Framework with Python:

1. Chatbots:

Use Case: Building a chatbot for customer support, FAQs, or order tracking.

Implementation:

- **Serverless Architecture**: Utilize AWS Lambda for chatbot logic, Amazon API Gateway for handling HTTP requests, and AWS DynamoDB for storing conversation history.

- **Natural Language Processing (NLP):** Integrate with NLP services like Amazon Lex or Google Dialogflow to understand user queries and generate appropriate responses.

```python
import boto3

def lambda_handler(event, context):
    # Process chatbot request
    user_message = event['message']
    # Implement NLP logic
    response = process_message(user_message)
    return {
```

```
    'statusCode': 200,
    'body': response
}
```

2. Image Processing:

Use Case: Automating image resizing, watermarking, or object detection for media assets.

Implementation:

- **Serverless Image Processing:** Use AWS Lambda with services like Amazon S3 and Amazon Rekognition to trigger image processing tasks on file uploads.

- **Asynchronous Processing:** Handle large-scale image processing tasks asynchronously using AWS Step Functions to coordinate multiple Lambda functions.

```python
import boto3

s3 = boto3.client('s3')
```

```
rekognition = boto3.client('rekognition')

def process_image(event, context):
    bucket_name = event['Records'][0]['s3']['bucket']['name']
    file_key = event['Records'][0]['s3']['object']['key']
    # Download image from S3
    image = download_image(bucket_name, file_key)
    # Perform image processing
    result = detect_objects(image)
    return result

def download_image(bucket_name, file_key):
    response = s3.get_object(Bucket=bucket_name, Key=file_key)
    return response['Body'].read()

def detect_objects(image):
    response = rekognition.detect_labels(Image={'Bytes': image})
    # Process detection results
    return response['Labels']
```

3. IoT:

Use Case: Monitoring and analyzing sensor data from IoT devices for predictive maintenance or environmental monitoring.

Implementation:

- **IoT Data Ingestion:** Use AWS IoT Core to securely ingest and process data from IoT devices.

- **Real-time Analytics:** Process and analyze IoT data in real-time using AWS Lambda and Amazon Kinesis for anomaly detection or predictive maintenance.

```python
import boto3

kinesis = boto3.client('kinesis')

def process_iot_data(event, context):
    # Process IoT data from Kinesis stream
    for record in event['Records']:
        data = record['kinesis']['data']
        # Decode and process data
        process_sensor_data(data)
```

```
def process_sensor_data(data):
    # Implement sensor data processing logic
    pass
```

Serverless computing offers a flexible and cost-effective approach to implementing various use cases such as chatbots, image processing, and IoT. By leveraging the Serverless Framework with Python and cloud services provided by AWS, developers can build scalable and resilient applications without managing infrastructure overhead. Whether it's building conversational interfaces, automating image manipulation tasks, or analyzing IoT data streams, serverless architecture empowers developers to focus on business logic and deliver value to end-users efficiently.

Chapter 14

Planning and strategizing your migration.

Planning and strategizing a migration involves careful consideration of various factors, including the current infrastructure, desired state, dependencies, and potential risks. When migrating applications to a serverless architecture using Python and frameworks like Serverless, there are several key steps to ensure a smooth transition. Let's break down the process into stages and discuss how Python and Serverless can be leveraged at each step.

1. Assessment and Inventory:

Before diving into migration, it's essential to understand the existing infrastructure, applications, and dependencies. Conduct an inventory of all applications, their components, and their dependencies. Tools like AWS Application Discovery Service can help identify dependencies.

```python
# Python script to assess current infrastructure
```

```python
import boto3

# Initialize AWS SDK
client = boto3.client('discovery')

# Get list of servers
response = client.describe_servers()

for server in response['servers']:
    print(f"Server Name: {server['server_name']}, IP Address: {server['server_ip_address']}")
```

2. Identify Candidate Applications:

Not all applications are suitable for serverless migration. Identify applications with intermittent or unpredictable workloads, stateless components, and well-defined inputs and outputs.

```python
# Identify candidate applications
candidate_applications = ['app1', 'app2', 'app3']
```

3. Select Serverless Providers and Frameworks:

Evaluate different serverless providers like AWS Lambda, Azure Functions, or Google Cloud Functions based on your requirements and constraints. Choose a serverless framework like Serverless Framework or AWS SAM to streamline deployment and management.

```python
# Select serverless provider and framework
serverless_provider = 'AWS Lambda'
serverless_framework = 'Serverless Framework'
```

4. Define Migration Strategy:

Based on the assessment, define the migration strategy. It could be a lift-and-shift approach for simple applications or a refactor-and-optimize approach for complex ones.

```python
# Define migration strategy
migration_strategy = 'Lift-and-Shift'
```

5. Architectural Design:

Design the architecture for the serverless applications, including function composition, event triggers, and data storage.

```python
# Architectural design
architectural_design = {
    'functions': {
        'function1': {
            'trigger': 'API Gateway',
            'runtime': 'Python 3.8'
        },
        'function2': {
            'trigger': 'S3',
            'runtime': 'Python 3.8'
        }
    },
    'data_storage': 'DynamoDB'
}
```

6. Refactor Codebase:

Refactor the existing codebase to adapt to the serverless architecture, focusing on modularization, statelessness, and event-driven design.

```python
# Refactor codebase
def lambda_handler(event, context):
    # Process event
    return {
        'statusCode': 200,
        'body': json.dumps('Hello from Lambda!')
    }
```

7. Implement CI/CD Pipeline:

Set up a continuous integration and continuous deployment pipeline using tools like AWS CodePipeline or Jenkins to automate the deployment process.

```python
# CI/CD pipeline configuration
pipeline_config = {
    'source': 'GitHub',
    'build': 'AWS CodeBuild',
    'deploy': 'AWS CodeDeploy'
```

}
```

## 8. Testing and Validation:

Thoroughly test the serverless applications, including unit tests, integration tests, and performance tests, to ensure functionality and reliability.

```python
# Testing and validation
def test_lambda_handler():
    event = {}
    context = {}
    assert lambda_handler(event, context) == {'statusCode': 200, 'body': '"Hello from Lambda!"'}
```

9. Security Considerations:

Implement security best practices for serverless applications, including least privilege access, input validation, and encryption at rest and in transit.

```python
# Security considerations
```
```

```
security_best_practices = {
    'least_privilege_access': True,
    'input_validation': True,
    'encryption': True
}
```

10. Monitoring and Logging:

Set up monitoring and logging for serverless applications using services like AWS CloudWatch to track performance, errors, and resource usage.

```python
# Monitoring and logging configuration
monitoring_logging_config = {
    'service': 'CloudWatch',
    'metrics': ['Invocations', 'Errors', 'Duration'],
    'logs': ['Lambda Logs']
}
```

11. Backup and Disaster Recovery:

Implement backup and disaster recovery mechanisms for critical data and applications to ensure business continuity.

```python
# Backup and disaster recovery
backup_disaster_recovery = {
    'data': 'Amazon S3 cross-region replication',
    'applications': 'AWS Backup'
}
```

12. Training and Documentation:

Provide training to the team on serverless concepts, best practices, and tools. Document the migration process, architecture, and configurations for future reference.

```python
# Training and documentation
training_documentation = {
    'serverless_concepts': ['Functions', 'Triggers', 'Events'],
    'best_practices': ['Scalability', 'Cost Optimization'],
    'tools': ['Serverless Framework', 'AWS Lambda']
}
```

Planning and strategizing migration to a serverless architecture using Python and frameworks like Serverless Framework require careful consideration of various aspects, including assessment, selection of providers and frameworks, architectural design, code refactoring, CI/CD setup, testing, security, monitoring, backup, and training. By following a structured approach and leveraging the power of Python and serverless technologies, organizations can achieve scalable, cost-effective, and resilient solutions.

Incremental migration techniques and best practices.

Incremental migration is a strategy where components of an application are migrated gradually, piece by piece, instead of attempting to move the entire application at once. This approach minimizes risks and allows for easier rollback if issues arise. When it comes to incremental migration with Python and the Serverless framework, there are several techniques and best practices to consider. Let's delve into them:

1. Monolithic to Microservices:

One common approach to incremental migration is breaking down a monolithic application into microservices. Each microservice can then be migrated independently to a serverless architecture.

```python
# Example: Monolithic to Microservices
# Original monolithic function
def monolithic_function(event, context):
    # Business logic
    return response

# Split into microservices
def microservice1(event, context):
    # Business logic for one feature
    return response1

def microservice2(event, context):
    # Business logic for another feature
    return response2
```

2. Strangler Fig Pattern:

In the strangler fig pattern, new functionality is implemented in a serverless architecture while gradually phasing out the old monolithic components.

```python
# Example: Strangler Fig Pattern
# Original monolithic function
def monolithic_function(event, context):
    if new_feature(event):
        # Call new serverless function
        return new_serverless_function(event, context)
    else:
        # Continue with monolithic logic
        return old_logic(event, context)

# New serverless function
def new_serverless_function(event, context):
    # Serverless implementation
    return new_response
```

3. Service Orchestration:

Leverage service orchestration tools like AWS Step Functions to coordinate serverless functions and manage complex workflows.

```python
# Example: Service Orchestration with AWS Step Functions
# Step Function definition
{
  "Comment": "Sample Step Function",
  "StartAt": "Lambda1",
  "States": {
   "Lambda1": {
    "Type": "Task",
    "Resource": "arn:aws:lambda:REGION:ACCOUNT_ID:function:FUNCTION_NAME",
    "Next": "Lambda2"
   },
   "Lambda2": {
    "Type": "Task",
    "Resource": "arn:aws:lambda:REGION:ACCOUNT_ID:function:FUNCTION_NAME",
    "End": true
}
```

4. **Feature Flags:**

Use feature flags to control the rollout of new serverless features, allowing for gradual testing and adoption.

```python
# Example: Feature Flags
if feature_enabled('new_feature'):
    # Call new serverless function
    response = new_serverless_function(event, context)
else:
    # Continue with old logic
    response = old_logic(event, context)
```

5. Blue-Green Deployment:

Implement blue-green deployments to seamlessly switch between old and new serverless environments for testing and production.

```python
# Example: Blue-Green Deployment
# Original function
def old_function(event, context):
    # Business logic
    return response
```

```python
# New function
def new_function(event, context):
    # Serverless implementation
    return new_response

# Switch between blue and green environments
if is_blue_environment():
    response = old_function(event, context)
else:
    response = new_function(event, context)
```

6. Traffic Shifting:

Gradually shift traffic from the old monolithic components to the new serverless functions using techniques like weighted routing.

```python
# Example: Traffic Shifting with Weighted Routing
# Original monolithic function
def monolithic_function(event, context):
    # Business logic
    return response
```

```python
# New serverless function
def new_serverless_function(event, context):
    # Serverless implementation
    return new_response

# Weighted routing configuration
if is_weighted_routing_enabled():
    if random.randint(1, 100) <= 80:  # 80% traffic to new function
        response = new_serverless_function(event, context)
    else:
        response = monolithic_function(event, context)
else:
    response = monolithic_function(event, context)  # Full traffic to monolithic function
```

7. Testing and Validation:

Thoroughly test each incremental change, including unit tests, integration tests, and end-to-end tests, to ensure functionality and compatibility.

```python
# Example: Testing and Validation
# Unit test for new serverless function
```

```
def test_new_serverless_function():
    event = {}
    context = {}
    assert new_serverless_function(event, context) == expected_response
```

8. Monitoring and Logging:

Monitor the performance and behavior of both the old monolithic components and the new serverless functions using tools like AWS CloudWatch.

```python
# Example: Monitoring and Logging
# CloudWatch configuration
{
  "MetricName": "Invocations",
  "Namespace": "AWS/Lambda",
  "Dimensions": [
    {
      "Name": "FunctionName",
      "Value": "new_serverless_function"
    }
  ],
  "Statistic": "Sum",
```

```
  "Period": 300,
  "Unit": "Count"
}
```

9. Rollback Strategy:

Have a rollback strategy in place to revert to the previous state if any issues or regressions occur during migration.

```python
# Example: Rollback Strategy
# If issue detected, switch back to old function
response = old_function(event, context)
```

Incremental migration techniques and best practices allow organizations to transition smoothly from monolithic architectures to serverless environments while minimizing risks and ensuring continuous delivery. By leveraging Python and the Serverless framework, developers can implement gradual changes, test thoroughly, monitor performance, and maintain flexibility throughout the migration process. With careful planning and execution, incremental migration can lead to scalable, efficient, and resilient applications in the serverless paradigm.

Common challenges and how to address them.

When migrating to a serverless architecture using Python and frameworks like Serverless, there are several common challenges that organizations may encounter. Understanding these challenges and implementing appropriate solutions is crucial for a successful migration. Let's explore some of these challenges and how to address them:

1. Cold Start Performance:

One of the primary challenges with serverless functions is the potential for cold starts, where the function takes longer to respond due to the initial setup time. This can impact user experience, especially for latency-sensitive applications.

Solution:

Implement techniques to minimize cold start times, such as optimizing code size, reducing dependencies, and using provisioned concurrency.

```python
# Example: Provisioned Concurrency Configuration
provider:
  name: aws
  runtime: python3.8
  provisionedConcurrency: 10  # Set to desired value
```

2. Vendor Lock-in:

Adopting a specific serverless provider can lead to vendor lock-in, making it challenging to switch to another provider in the future.

Solution:

Use abstraction layers and standardize interfaces to decouple applications from specific cloud providers. Adopt serverless frameworks like Serverless Framework or AWS SAM that support multiple providers.

```python
```

```
# Example: Serverless Framework Configuration
provider:
  name: aws  # Or other supported providers
  runtime: python3.8
```

3. Limited Debugging and Monitoring Tools:

Serverless environments may have limited debugging and monitoring tools compared to traditional architectures, making it difficult to troubleshoot issues.

Solution:

Leverage third-party monitoring and logging services like AWS CloudWatch, Datadog, or New Relic. Instrument code with logging statements and use distributed tracing for better visibility into function execution.

```python
# Example: Logging Configuration
import logging

logger = logging.getLogger()
logger.setLevel(logging.INFO)
```

```python
def lambda_handler(event, context):
    logger.info('Received event: %s', event)
    # Business logic
```

4. Dependency Management:

Managing dependencies in serverless functions can be challenging, especially when dealing with conflicting versions or large dependency trees.

Solution:

Use lightweight dependencies and minimize external dependencies where possible. Utilize tools like pipenv or poetry for dependency management and version pinning.

```python
# Example: Dependency Management with Pipenv
# Create Pipfile
[[source]]
name = "pypi"
url = "https://pypi.org/simple"
verify_ssl = true
```

```
[packages]
requests = "*"

[dev-packages]

[requires]
python_version = "3.8"
```

5. Scalability Limits:

While serverless architectures offer scalability benefits, they have inherent limits, such as maximum concurrent executions and resource quotas.

Solution:

Design applications for horizontal scalability by breaking down functionality into smaller, independent functions. Monitor usage patterns and adjust resource configurations accordingly.

```python
# Example: Resource Configuration
provider:
  name: aws
```

```
runtime: python3.8
memorySize: 1024  # Adjust as needed
timeout: 30  # Adjust as needed
```

6. State Management:

Serverless functions are typically stateless, which can pose challenges for applications that require stateful interactions.

Solution:

Leverage external data stores like databases (e.g., DynamoDB, RDS) or cache systems (e.g., Redis) for storing and managing state. Use session tokens or client-side storage for maintaining user sessions.

```python
# Example: DynamoDB Integration
import boto3

dynamodb = boto3.resource('dynamodb')
table = dynamodb.Table('my_table')

def lambda_handler(event, context):
```

```
# Retrieve or update state in DynamoDB
```

7. Security Concerns:

Serverless environments introduce unique security challenges, including data exposure, privilege escalation, and insecure configurations.

Solution:

Follow security best practices such as least privilege access, input validation, encryption, and secure configuration management. Implement authentication and authorization mechanisms to control access to serverless functions.

```python
# Example: Authorization with IAM
# Define IAM role with appropriate permissions
# Attach IAM role to serverless function
```

8. Deployment Complexity:

Deploying serverless applications can be complex, involving multiple configurations, dependencies, and environment setups.

Solution:

Automate deployment processes using CI/CD pipelines with tools like AWS CodePipeline, GitHub Actions, or Jenkins. Utilize infrastructure as code (IaC) to define and manage serverless resources.

```python
# Example: CI/CD Pipeline Configuration
# Define pipeline stages for build, test, and deploy
# Integrate with version control system for automated deployments
```

Migrating to a serverless architecture using Python and frameworks like Serverless offers numerous benefits, but it also comes with its own set of challenges. By understanding these challenges and implementing appropriate solutions, organizations can mitigate risks, optimize performance, and ensure a smooth transition to serverless computing. From optimizing cold start times to managing dependencies and ensuring security, addressing these challenges requires careful planning, continuous monitoring, and proactive optimization strategies. With the right approach and tools, serverless migration can unlock new levels of scalability, efficiency, and agility for modern applications.

Tools and frameworks to facilitate migration.

When embarking on a migration to a serverless architecture with Python, leveraging the right tools and frameworks can significantly streamline the process, improve efficiency, and ensure success. Let's explore some of the top tools and frameworks available to facilitate migration and development in the serverless ecosystem:

1. Serverless Framework:

The Serverless Framework is a popular open-source framework that simplifies building, deploying, and managing serverless applications across multiple cloud providers.

```python
# Example: Serverless Framework Configuration
# serverless.yml
```

```
service: my-service

provider:
  name: aws
  runtime: python3.8

functions:
  hello:
    handler: handler.hello
```

2. AWS SAM (Serverless Application Model):

AWS SAM is an extension of CloudFormation that simplifies the development and deployment of serverless applications on AWS.

```python
# Example: AWS SAM Configuration
# template.yaml
Resources:
  HelloWorldFunction:
    Type: AWS::Serverless::Function
    Properties:
      Handler: handler.hello
      Runtime: python3.8
```

```

### 3. Boto3:

Boto3 is the official AWS SDK for Python, providing easy-to-use APIs for interacting with various AWS services, such as Lambda, DynamoDB, S3, and more.

```python
# Example: Boto3 Usage
import boto3

lambda_client = boto3.client('lambda')

response = lambda_client.invoke(
    FunctionName='my-function',
    InvocationType='RequestResponse',
    Payload='{}'
)
```

4. AWS CDK (Cloud Development Kit):

AWS CDK is an infrastructure as code framework that allows developers to define cloud infrastructure using
```

familiar programming languages like Python, TypeScript, and Java.

```python
# Example: AWS CDK Python
from aws_cdk import core
from aws_cdk.aws_lambda import Function, Runtime

class MyStack(core.Stack):

    def __init__(self, scope: core.Construct, id: str, **kwargs) -> None:
        super().__init__(scope, id, **kwargs)

        Function(
            self, 'MyFunction',
            runtime=Runtime.PYTHON_3_8,
            handler='index.handler',
            code='path/to/lambda/code'
        )
```

5. Pulumi:

Pulumi is another infrastructure as code tool that supports multiple cloud providers, including AWS,

Azure, and Google Cloud Platform, using familiar programming languages.

```python
# Example: Pulumi Python
import pulumi
import pulumi_aws as aws

lambda_function = aws.lambda_.Function(
    'my-function',
    runtime='python3.8',
    handler='handler.hello',
    code=pulumi.AssetArchive({
        '.': pulumi.FileArchive('path/to/lambda/code')
    })
)
```

6. Terraform:

Terraform is a widely used infrastructure as code tool that supports multiple cloud providers, including AWS, Azure, and Google Cloud Platform.

```hcl
# Example: Terraform AWS Lambda
```

```
resource "aws_lambda_function" "my_function" {
  function_name = "my-function"
  handler = "handler.hello"
  runtime = "python3.8"
  filename = "path/to/lambda/code.zip"
}
```

7. LocalStack:

LocalStack is a tool for running AWS cloud services locally for development and testing purposes, allowing developers to emulate AWS services on their local machine.

```python
# Example: LocalStack with Python
from localstack.services import infra

# Start LocalStack
infra.start_localstack()

# Use Boto3 to interact with local AWS services
import boto3
```

```
lambda_client = boto3.client('lambda',
endpoint_url='http://localhost:4566')

response = lambda_client.list_functions()
```

8. SAM Local:

SAM Local is a CLI tool for locally testing and debugging serverless applications built with AWS SAM.

```bash
# Example: SAM Local Invocation
sam local invoke MyFunction --event event.json
```

9. Docker:

Docker containers are useful for packaging and running serverless functions locally, ensuring consistency between development and production environments.

```Dockerfile
# Example: Dockerfile for Python Lambda
FROM public.ecr.aws/lambda/python:3.8
```

```
COPY app.py ./

CMD ["app.handler"]
```

10. AWS CodePipeline:

AWS CodePipeline is a continuous integration and continuous deployment service that automates the build, test, and deployment phases of your release process.

```yaml
# Example: AWS CodePipeline Configuration
# pipeline.yml
Stages:
  - Name: Source
    Actions:
      - Name: SourceAction
        ActionTypeId:
          Category: Source
          Owner: AWS
          Version: 1
          Provider: CodeCommit
        Configuration:
          RepositoryName: MyRepo
          BranchName: master
```

```
      OutputArtifacts:
        - Name: MyApp

  - Name: Deploy
    Actions:
      - Name: DeployAction
        ActionTypeId:
          Category: Deploy
          Owner: AWS
          Version: 1
          Provider: Lambda
        Configuration:
          FunctionName: MyFunction
        InputArtifacts:
          - Name: MyApp
```

Migrating to a serverless architecture with Python requires careful planning, development, and deployment using the right set of tools and frameworks. Whether it's using Serverless Framework, AWS SAM, Boto3, or infrastructure as code tools like AWS CDK, Terraform, or Pulumi, having the right tooling can significantly simplify the migration process, improve developer productivity, and ensure consistency across environments. Additionally, tools like LocalStack, SAM

Local, Docker, and AWS CodePipeline provide invaluable support for local development, testing, and automation of deployment pipelines. By leveraging these tools effectively, organizations can successfully migrate to serverless architectures with Python and unlock the benefits of scalability, agility, and cost-efficiency.

Conclusion

In conclusion, mastering the Python Serverless framework opens up a world of possibilities for developers to build scalable, efficient, and resilient applications. By harnessing the power of serverless computing, developers can focus on writing code without the burden of managing infrastructure, leading to increased productivity and faster time to market.

With the Serverless framework, developers can leverage a wide range of advanced features and best practices to streamline their development process. From implementing code reusability and efficiency techniques to designing robust error handling and state management strategies, the Serverless framework empowers developers to architect solutions that meet the demands of modern cloud-native applications.

Furthermore, the Serverless framework provides seamless integration with various cloud services, enabling developers to leverage a rich ecosystem of tools and services for tasks such as data processing, storage, authentication, and monitoring. Whether it's deploying functions triggered by HTTP requests, processing streaming data in real-time, or orchestrating complex workflows with state machines, the Serverless framework offers a flexible and scalable platform for building diverse applications.

As organizations increasingly adopt serverless architectures, mastering the Python Serverless framework becomes a valuable skill for developers looking to stay ahead in the rapidly evolving tech landscape. By honing their expertise in serverless development, developers can unlock new opportunities for innovation, collaboration, and growth, while delivering exceptional value to their users and stakeholders.

In summary, mastering the Python Serverless framework empowers developers to unleash their creativity, accelerate their development workflow, and build cutting-edge applications that scale effortlessly and delight users. With its intuitive syntax, rich ecosystem, and powerful features, the Serverless framework is the tool of choice for modern developers looking to build the next generation of cloud-native applications.

Appendix

A: Glossary of Serverless Terms

Here's a glossary of serverless terms based on mastering Python Serverless framework:

1. Serverless Computing: Serverless computing is a cloud computing model where cloud providers dynamically manage the allocation and provisioning of servers, allowing developers to focus on writing code without worrying about infrastructure management.

2. Function-as-a-Service (FaaS): Function-as-a-Service (FaaS) is a category of serverless computing where developers deploy individual functions that are triggered by events. These functions are short-lived and stateless, executing specific tasks in response to events such as HTTP requests, database changes, or timer triggers.

3. Serverless Framework: The Serverless Framework is an open-source framework that simplifies the deployment and management of serverless applications. It provides tools, plugins, and abstractions to help developers build, deploy, and maintain serverless functions across different cloud providers.

4. AWS Lambda: AWS Lambda is a FaaS offering from Amazon Web Services (AWS) that allows developers to run code without provisioning or managing servers. With Lambda, developers can deploy functions written in various programming languages, including Python, and scale them automatically in response to incoming events.

5. Event-Driven Architecture: Event-driven architecture is a design pattern where components within an application communicate asynchronously through events. In serverless computing, functions are triggered by events such as HTTP requests, message queue events, or database changes, allowing for decoupled and scalable architectures.

6. Cold Start: A cold start refers to the initial invocation of a serverless function where the cloud provider needs to allocate resources and initialize the execution environment. Cold starts can introduce latency, especially for functions that are infrequently invoked, but can be mitigated through techniques such as pre-warming or optimizing function code.

7. Warm Start: A warm start occurs when a serverless function is invoked and there are already resources allocated and an execution environment initialized, resulting in lower latency compared to cold starts. Warm starts are beneficial for functions with frequent invocations or time-sensitive workloads.

8. Triggers: Triggers are events that cause serverless functions to execute. Triggers can be various types, including HTTP requests, database changes, file uploads, or timer-based events. Serverless functions are designed to respond to specific triggers and execute corresponding logic.

9. Orchestration: Orchestration is the coordination of multiple serverless functions or services to accomplish complex workflows. With orchestration tools like AWS Step Functions, developers can define workflows that coordinate the execution of multiple functions in a sequential or parallel manner, enabling the construction of sophisticated applications.

10. State Management: State management involves maintaining the state of serverless functions across invocations. External storage services such as databases or object storage are often used to persist and manage state, ensuring consistency and durability across function executions.

11. Fault Tolerance: Fault tolerance is the ability of a serverless application to continue operating in the presence of failures or errors. Serverless architectures are inherently fault-tolerant due to their distributed and event-driven nature, but developers can further enhance fault tolerance through techniques such as error handling, retries, and circuit breakers.

12. Scalability: Scalability refers to the ability of a serverless application to handle varying workloads by dynamically scaling resources up or down in response to demand. Serverless platforms automatically scale functions based on incoming events, allowing applications to handle thousands or even millions of requests without manual intervention.

13. Observability: Observability is the ability to understand and monitor the internal state of a serverless application. Observability tools and techniques such as logging, metrics, and distributed tracing help developers gain insights into the performance, behavior, and health of their serverless functions, facilitating troubleshooting, optimization, and performance tuning.

Understanding these serverless terms is essential for developers looking to master the Python Serverless framework and build scalable, efficient, and resilient applications in the cloud. By leveraging the capabilities of serverless computing and adopting best practices, developers can unlock new opportunities for innovation and deliver exceptional value to their users and stakeholders.

B: Serverless Framework Configuration Options (YAML and Python)

Configuring a serverless application is a crucial aspect of building robust and scalable serverless functions. The Serverless Framework provides powerful configuration options using YAML and Python, allowing developers to define various aspects of their serverless application, including function properties, resources, environment variables, and more. Let's delve into these configuration options and provide examples using both YAML and Python formats.

1. YAML Configuration: YAML is a human-readable data serialization format commonly used for configuring serverless applications with the Serverless Framework. Here's an overview of some key configuration options:

a. Service Configuration:

```yaml
# serverless.yml

service: my-service
provider:
  name: aws
```

```
  runtime: python3.8
  stage: dev
  region: us-east-1
```

In this example, we define basic service configuration options such as the service name, provider (AWS), runtime (Python 3.8), stage, and region.

b. Function Configuration:

```yaml
# serverless.yml

functions:
  my_function:
    handler: handler.my_function
    events:
      - http:
          path: my-function
          method: get
```

Here, we define a serverless function named `my_function` with its handler function (`handler.my_function`) and an HTTP event trigger.

c. Environment Variables:

```yaml
# serverless.yml

provider:
  environment:
    MY_ENV_VAR: my_value
```

This configuration sets environment variables for the entire service. You can also specify environment variables at the function level.

d. Resources:

```yaml
# serverless.yml

resources:
  Resources:
    MyDynamoDBTable:
      Type: AWS::DynamoDB::Table
      Properties:
        TableName: MyTable
```

```
      AttributeDefinitions:
        - AttributeName: id
          AttributeType: S
      KeySchema:
        - AttributeName: id
          KeyType: HASH
      ProvisionedThroughput:
        ReadCapacityUnits: 5
        WriteCapacityUnits: 5
```

This example defines an AWS DynamoDB table as a CloudFormation resource within the Serverless Framework configuration.

2. Python Configuration: In addition to YAML, the Serverless Framework supports configuring your application using Python code. Here's how you can achieve the same configurations using Python:

a. Service Configuration:

```python
# serverless.py

from serverless_sdk import handler_wrapper
```

```
def handler(context):
    return handler_wrapper(_handler)

def _handler(event, context):
    return {"statusCode": 200, "body": "Hello, World!"}
```

In this Python configuration, we define a simple serverless function handler using the `serverless_sdk`.

b. Function Configuration:

```python
# serverless.py

def my_function(event, context):
    return {"statusCode": 200, "body": "Hello, World!"}

my_function.events = [
    {
        "http": {
            "path": "my-function",
            "method": "get"
        }
```

Here, we define the function `my_function` along with its HTTP event trigger using Python decorators.

c. Environment Variables:

```python
# serverless.py

def my_function(event, context):
    my_env_var = os.environ.get('MY_ENV_VAR')
    return {"statusCode": 200, "body": f"Value of MY_ENV_VAR: {my_env_var}"}
```

Environment variables can be accessed directly within your Python code using `os.environ`.

d. Resources:

The Serverless Framework Python SDK doesn't directly support defining CloudFormation resources within Python code. For resource definitions, it's recommended to use YAML configuration.

Configuring a serverless application using YAML and Python with the Serverless Framework provides flexibility and ease of use for developers. Whether you prefer the declarative nature of YAML or the programmatic capabilities of Python, the Serverless Framework offers powerful options for defining your serverless architecture, managing resources, setting environment variables, and more. Understanding these configuration options is essential for mastering the Serverless Framework and building scalable and efficient serverless applications.

C: Troubleshooting Common Serverless Framework Issues

Troubleshooting common issues with the Serverless Framework is an essential skill for developers working with serverless applications. In this guide, we'll explore some common problems encountered when using the Serverless Framework with Python and provide solutions and best practices for troubleshooting these issues effectively.

1. Deployment Failures:

Deployment failures can occur due to various reasons such as configuration errors, resource limitations, or network issues. Here are some steps to troubleshoot deployment failures:

a. Check Configuration:

Ensure that your `serverless.yml` or `serverless.py` configuration is correct, including service, provider, function, and resource definitions. Verify that all required fields are provided and that there are no syntax errors in your configuration files.

Example:

```yaml
# serverless.yml

service: my-service
provider:
  name: aws
  runtime: python3.8
  stage: dev
  region: us-east-1

functions:
  my_function:
    handler: handler.my_function
    events:
      - http:
          path: my-function
          method: get
```

b. Check Cloud Provider Limits:

Check the limits imposed by your cloud provider (e.g., AWS Lambda) on resources such as function memory, execution time, and deployment package size. Make sure your functions comply with these limits to avoid deployment failures.

c. Review Deployment Logs:

Review the deployment logs provided by the Serverless Framework to identify any errors or warnings encountered during the deployment process. Look for specific error messages that can help diagnose the root cause of the deployment failure.

2. Cold Start Performance:

Cold starts can lead to increased latency for serverless function invocations, especially for functions that are infrequently invoked. Here are some strategies to mitigate cold start performance issues:

a. Optimize Function Code:

Optimize your function code to reduce cold start times by minimizing dependencies, reducing function size, and improving initialization logic. Consider using lightweight frameworks and libraries to decrease startup time.

Example:

```python
# serverless.py

from serverless_sdk import handler_wrapper

def handler(context):
    return handler_wrapper(_handler)

def _handler(event, context):
    return {"statusCode": 200, "body": "Hello, World!"}
```

b. Provisioned Concurrency:

Use provisioned concurrency to pre-warm your functions and keep them ready to handle incoming requests, thereby reducing cold start latency. Configure provisioned concurrency settings in your serverless configuration to ensure consistent performance.

c. Warm-Up Requests:

Implement warm-up requests by periodically invoking your functions with dummy requests to keep them warm.

You can use scheduling services like AWS CloudWatch Events to trigger warm-up requests at regular intervals.

3. Resource Limit Exceeded Errors:

Resource limit exceeded errors can occur when your serverless functions exceed the limits imposed by your cloud provider. Here's how to address these errors:

a. Increase Limits:

If you encounter resource limit exceeded errors, consider increasing the limits imposed by your cloud provider for resources such as function memory, concurrent executions, or deployment package size. Reach out to your cloud provider's support team for assistance with increasing limits.

b. Optimize Resource Usage:

Optimize your serverless functions to reduce resource usage by minimizing memory footprint, optimizing code execution, and limiting the use of external resources such as database connections and network requests. Use monitoring and profiling tools to identify resource-intensive operations and optimize them for efficiency.

4. Debugging Function Execution:

Debugging serverless functions can be challenging due to the distributed and event-driven nature of serverless architectures. Here are some techniques for debugging function execution issues:

a. Logging:

Use logging statements within your function code to capture debugging information, including input parameters, intermediate results, and error messages. Configure logging levels and log aggregation services to ensure comprehensive visibility into function execution.

Example:

```python
# serverless.py

import logging

logger = logging.getLogger(__name__)

def my_function(event, context):
```

```
logger.info("Received event: %s", event)
    ...
```

b. Cloud Provider Tools:

Leverage cloud provider tools such as AWS CloudWatch Logs, Azure Application Insights, or Google Cloud Logging to monitor and analyze function execution logs in real-time. Use built-in features such as log streaming and log search to troubleshoot issues effectively.

c. Local Debugging:

Use local development and debugging tools provided by the Serverless Framework to simulate function execution environments locally. Test your functions with sample inputs and debug them using breakpoints, step-through debugging, and interactive consoles.

Example:

```bash
serverless invoke local -f my_function --data '{"key": "value"}'
```

```

Troubleshooting common issues with the Serverless Framework requires a systematic approach and familiarity with serverless architectures, cloud provider services, and development best practices. By following the strategies outlined in this guide, developers can effectively diagnose and resolve deployment failures, cold start performance issues, resource limit exceeded errors, and function execution bugs, ensuring the reliability and performance of their serverless applications. Additionally, continuous monitoring, testing, and optimization are essential for maintaining the health and scalability of serverless applications over time.
```

D: Best Practices Checklist for Python Serverless Development

Python, coupled with the Serverless Framework, offers a powerful combination for building scalable and efficient serverless applications. To ensure success in your Python serverless development endeavors, follow this comprehensive best practices checklist:

1. Optimize Function Size and Initialization:

- **Minimize Dependencies:** Reduce the number and size of dependencies to decrease deployment package size and cold start times.

- **Lazy Initialization:** Delay initialization of resources until they are needed to reduce cold start latency.

- **Use Lightweight Frameworks:** Choose lightweight frameworks and libraries to minimize function size and improve performance.

```python
# Example: Minimizing Dependencies
# Instead of importing unnecessary modules:
```

```
# import pandas as pd
# import numpy as np

# Only import required modules:
import json
import requests
```

2. Leverage Provisioned Concurrency:

- **Pre-Warm Functions:** Use provisioned concurrency to keep functions warm and ready to handle incoming requests, reducing cold start latency and improving performance.

- **Configure Provisioned Concurrency:** Set up provisioned concurrency settings in your serverless configuration to ensure consistent performance for critical functions.

```yaml
# Example: Provisioned Concurrency Configuration
provider:
  name: aws
  ...
  provisionedConcurrency: 5
```

```

## 3. Implement Error Handling and Logging:

- **Handle Exceptions Gracefully:** Implement error handling logic to catch and handle exceptions gracefully, providing meaningful error messages to users.

- **Use Structured Logging:** Utilize structured logging to capture detailed information about function execution, including input parameters, intermediate results, and error messages.

```python
# Example: Error Handling and Logging
import logging

logger = logging.getLogger(__name__)

def my_function(event, context):
    try:
        # Function logic
        ...
    except Exception as e:
        # Log the exception with detailed information

```
        logger.error('An error occurred', exc_info=True,
extra={'event': event, 'context': context})
        return {
            'statusCode': 500,
            'body': 'Internal Server Error'
        }
```

4. Optimize Resource Usage:

- **Right-Size Resources:** Optimize resource allocation such as memory, CPU, and storage to match the requirements of your functions, avoiding over-provisioning and unnecessary costs.

- **Reuse Connections:** Reuse database connections, HTTP connections, and other resources to minimize overhead and improve performance.

```python
# Example: Reusing Database Connections
import boto3

dynamodb = boto3.resource('dynamodb')
```

```
def my_function(event, context):
    table = dynamodb.Table('my_table')
```

5. Monitor Performance and Health:

- **Use Monitoring Tools:** Utilize monitoring and observability tools such as AWS CloudWatch, Azure Application Insights, or Google Cloud Monitoring to track function performance, detect anomalies, and troubleshoot issues.

- **Set Alarms:** Configure alarms to notify you of performance degradation, errors, or resource exhaustion, enabling proactive monitoring and remediation.

```yaml
# Example: CloudWatch Alarms Configuration
provider:
  name: aws
  ...
  alarms:
    - name: LambdaErrors
      type: CloudWatchAlarm
```

description: Alarm for Lambda errors
```

## 6. Secure Your Application:

- **Implement Least Privilege:** Follow the principle of least privilege when assigning permissions to serverless functions, limiting access to only the resources and actions they require.

- **Encrypt Sensitive Data:** Encrypt sensitive data at rest and in transit using encryption libraries and services provided by your cloud provider.

```python
# Example: Encrypting Sensitive Data
import boto3
from botocore.exceptions import ClientError

def encrypt_data(data):
    kms = boto3.client('kms')
    try:
        response = kms.encrypt(
            KeyId='my-key-id',
            Plaintext=data

        )
        return response['CiphertextBlob']
    except ClientError as e:
        print(f"Error encrypting data: {e}")
        return None
```

7. **Test Thoroughly:**

    - **Unit Testing:** Write unit tests for individual functions to validate their behavior and functionality.

    - **Integration Testing:** Perform integration tests to ensure that serverless functions interact correctly with other components and services in the application.

```python
# Example: Unit Testing with pytest
def test_my_function():
    event = {...}
    context = {...}
    assert my_function(event, context) == {...}
```
```

8. Optimize Costs:

- **Monitor Usage and Costs:** Monitor resource usage and associated costs using cloud provider billing and cost management tools to identify opportunities for optimization.

- **Implement Cost Controls:** Implement cost controls such as budget alerts and resource quotas to prevent unexpected cost overruns.

```yaml
# Example: AWS Budgets Configuration
provider:
  name: aws
  ...
  budget:
    amount: 100.0
    unit: USD
    period: month
```

9. Automate Deployment and CI/CD:

- **Use Infrastructure as Code (IaC):** Define your serverless infrastructure using configuration files

(YAML or Python) to enable versioning, reproducibility, and automation.

- **Continuous Integration/Continuous Deployment (CI/CD):** Implement CI/CD pipelines to automate the deployment process, ensuring fast and reliable delivery of changes to production.

```yaml
# Example: CI/CD Pipeline Configuration
provider:
  name: aws
  ...
  deploymentBucket:
    name: my-deployment-bucket
  ...
  deploymentPreference:
    type: canary10Percent10Minutes
```

10. Document Your Architecture:

- **Document Architecture:** Document your serverless architecture, including function design, event sources, dependencies, and interactions, to facilitate understanding, collaboration, and troubleshooting.

- **Version Documentation:** Versions control your documentation along with your codebase to ensure consistency and traceability.

```markdown
# Example: Architecture Documentation
## Function: my_function

- **Description**: Process incoming events from API Gateway.

- **Event Source:** HTTP event trigger.

- **Dependencies**: DynamoDB, S3.
```

By adhering to this best practices checklist for Python serverless development, you can build robust, scalable, and efficient serverless applications with confidence. Whether you're optimizing function size and initialization, leveraging provisioned concurrency, implementing error handling and logging, optimizing resource usage, monitoring performance and health, securing your application, testing thoroughly, optimizing costs, automating deployment and CI/CD, or documenting your architecture, following these best practices will set you on the path to success in your Python serverless development endeavors.